Chamique

On Family, Focus, and Basketball

Chamique Holdsclaw

with Jennifer Frey

SCRIBNER

NEW YORK LONDON TORONTO SYDNEY SINGAPORE

SCRIBNER
1230 Avenue of the Americas
New York, NY 10020

SCRIBNER and design are trademarks of Macmillan Library
Reference USA, Inc., used under license by Simon & Schuster,
the publisher of this work.

Designed by Colin Joh
Text set in New Baskerville

Manufactured in the United States of America

1 3 5 7 9 10 8 6 4 2

Library of Congress Cataloging-in-Publication Data is available.

ISBN 0-7432-0220-1

All photos courtesy of Chamique Holdsclaw.

To my grandmother, June Holdsclaw,
who has been the rock for my family and for me,
for raising me to believe that
I could accomplish anything

Acknowledgments

Special thanks to my family, who raised and supported me: my grandmother, June Holdsclaw; my mother, Bonita Holdsclaw; my father, Willie Johnson; my brother, Davon; my aunt Anita Holdsclaw and my uncle George Dells. To my little cousins—Thurman Holdsclaw Jr. and Kassala Holdsclaw, the children of my late uncle Thurman, who first handed me a basketball—I hope this book helps you realize that any dream can come true if only you believe.

Thanks to my coaches at Christ the King High School and Tennessee for helping me learn this game that I love, with special thanks to Coach Pat Summitt for her guidance. My heartfelt gratitude to all those who contributed their thoughts and memories to this book—your voices were invaluable in telling my story. Thanks to Lon Babby, Bob Barnett, Jim Tanner, and all the helpful people at Williams & Connolly for their constant guidance. And, finally, thanks to Sarah McGrath at Scribner for making this book a reality despite the incredible time restraints.

Jennifer Frey would like to thank her agent, Andrew Blauner, and her editors and colleagues at *The Washington Post*.

Chamique

Chapter 1

*Chamique, age four, celebrates Christmas
at her grandmother's apartment.*

My story always begins in Astoria, in the housing project in Queens where I grew up playing ball with the guys, my grandmother watching out for me through a bedroom window in our apartment. When people write stories about me, they always call it something of a desolate place, my building one of a bunch of battered-looking high-rises grouped together along the East River, with the basketball courts in the center. There's a lot of graffiti, and I suppose a lot of drugs, if you wanted them and knew where to look. I never did, and no one ever bothered me.

It wasn't a pretty place, but that's not something I really noticed. To me it was just home, the best home I'd ever had. I had the basketball courts just a few steps outside the front door of my building, a bus stop, a few stores nearby. So the building was old, the metal door scarred by bullets, the walls and floors cold cement. I never rode the elevator, because I was always afraid of getting stuck inside. Besides, it was lazy. Our apartment was up one short flight of stairs, then around the corner. Apartment 1-D. It was home.

It's a cozy apartment, three bedrooms, twin beds in my room, with a window overlooking the courts. My grandmother always made it nice. She had pictures everywhere, and rose petals in bowls, and all those little things that make you forget the chipped paint and old linoleum. My grandmother's friend Miss Jenny lived across the hall. My friend Anthony lived there too, on the same floor. The neighbors all watched out for me and for my grandmother. They still do.

I know what it must look like to outsiders, and what they must think when they see my neighborhood for the first time. When Coach Pat Summitt and her assistant, Mickie DeMoss, came from Tennessee to recruit me, Coach Vinny Cannizzaro—my high school coach—walked them from their car to my building, sure that two Southern ladies in heels and suits would get a hard time in my neighborhood. Of course, he was right. They heard some whistles, some trash talk. That was just the way people were there, wary of outsiders on their turf.

Mickie says that when she got into the elevator and saw the profanity scrawled on the walls and an empty beer can on the floor, she was horrified. *This is what Chamique has to look at every day?* she thought. She knew right away that she had to get me out of that environment. "All I wanted to do," Mickie tells me now, "was take you away from that building and back to Tennessee, where we could give you structure and discipline and an environment that was safe." I think she and Coach Summitt thought they could save me or something. And they did give me perhaps the most amazing opportunity of my life. Playing for Tennessee was one of the greatest things that ever happened to me, and playing for Coach Summitt, hard as it was at times, made me so much better a basketball player and so much stronger a person.

But what Mickie didn't understand that day—what almost no one understood—is that going to live in that housing project with my grandmother *is* what saved me. It was my escape. It was the place where I learned discipline, and it was the first place where I learned to feel safe. It was home, and still is. I've always been pretty happy. That's the thing that's hard for me to understand, and explain, sometimes. I never wanted for anything. My brother, Davon, and I, we never went without clothes. We had shoes on our feet. We had people who cared for us. It was just our situation that made me angry and frustrated. I never wanted for anything, but I know what it's like to grow up without two parents. To have to go and live with your grandmother because your parents aren't going to be there for you. To watch your family fall apart.

Sometimes it seems like the only thing people know about me is that I bounce this basketball and I'm from Astoria. I'm a simple little rags-to-riches story, one that has been told about NBA players from the projects for years. That's too simplistic. People who believe that story don't know me as a person. They don't know what drives me, what motivates me, what pushes me. They don't know where I'm from, beyond this little square of asphalt in Astoria. They think: *What pushes her is she's from the Astoria projects.* They don't see beyond that. Probably because they can't see inside me.

What pushes me is my brother, Davon, and what I want for him—what I want him to believe. I want to see him grow up safe. I want to see my family in a good situation after having been through so much bad. I want Davon to know—I want everyone to know—that just because your life seems dark, that doesn't mean there isn't a way out. There's a positive on the other side, if you look hard enough. And you can change things, if you try hard enough. That's what I want to show Davon. That's what I want to show everyone.

A lot of times I look at what I have been through, and where I am now, and the way I have evolved and changed, and I think: *This is what shaped me.* No matter how much people say, "Oh, it doesn't matter where you come from," it does matter. It mattered for me.

But as much as I come from Astoria Houses, I also come from a small apartment in a high-rise building in Jamaica, Queens. That's where I lived with my mother, Bonita, and my father, William Johnson, until I was eleven years old. That apartment is where I learned to be strong and independent. That is where I learned to survive. That is where I became, in large part, the person I am today.

My mother was nineteen years old when she had me, and she was twenty-two when she and my dad had my brother, Davon. I love them both, and I love my brother with a fierceness I can hardly explain. Family is so important to me. But my parents

13

weren't ready to raise kids—not me, and not my brother. They had their own lives to figure out, their own demons to fight. So Davon and I, we became our own little family. I was the mom, he was the kid. We held each other tight at night when things got scary, and he looked to me to bring him dinner, to watch over him, to take care of him, no matter what. I did the best I could. And I'm still trying. Davon is starting college now, and that's always been my hope for him—that he would find something to drive him the way I found basketball. I've always wanted him to realize that no matter how bad things were for us and our family in the beginning, we can end up blessed. He can end up blessed.

When we went to live at my grandmother's apartment—when I was eleven and Davon was eight—it wasn't because my mother felt it would be best for us. We went because Children's Services decided we could no longer live in the environment that existed inside that apartment in Jamaica. It broke my heart to see the cops come, and then to have our caseworker tell me that we couldn't live with our parents anymore. I didn't want to stop being a family. It was the only thing I knew. Later, when I was thirteen and Davon was ten, he went back to live with my mother and I chose to stay with my grandmother, and I felt that loss of family all over again.

So many people want to believe that it was basketball that got me out of the projects, that it was basketball that saved me. I don't believe that. I think it was my grandmother who saved me. And it was the strength I found in myself those years in Jamaica that gave me the drive and focus to make something of my life, with basketball or without. I have to believe that I would have gone to college even without my jump shot. I would have gotten my degree, started my life, become someone. I've never been a weak individual, I've always been pretty strong. I've always had to be.

I know that basketball has given me a life better than anything I could ever have imagined. I've graduated from a wonderful college, earned three national championships. I've had so many outlets. I have traveled around the world, played for the U.S. national team, had the opportunity to win a gold medal for my country in the world championships. I'm going to Sydney to play in the Olympics. I feel blessed, having the things I do. I'm able to get myself a car and a place to live, and I'm able to help my family in ways I never imagined. I could give my grandmother anything she wants, if only she'd let me. But she never asks for anything. She never has.

I love playing basketball. In a sense, it's always been my cushion. The court was a place for me to take out my anger and frustrations without risking trouble or hurting someone else. It was my comfort zone. It was also a place where I always knew my abilities, trusted in myself.

It's harder, I've learned, to find that kind of comfort and trust in the rest of your life. That's where I've struggled.

Sometimes people think I'm boring, because I really don't like to go to parties or clubs. I'd rather hang out at home with my friends and watch a movie or something like that. And people have made fun of me because I don't drink—okay, I'll have an occasional glass of champagne—and I don't smoke and I don't do drugs. They tease me because my main curse word is "Dag!" (though I've been known to use something a little stronger when I'm really ticked off) and because I never had a boyfriend until college. My high school teammate and good friend Kristeena Alexander still likes to tell people, "Chamique was never macking with no boys." It's not that I wasn't interested, but I had a life. I had things to do. I had goals. I had basketball.

When I was in junior high, the girls in the neighborhood used to make fun of me for spending all my time on the basketball court, playing with the boys. I wasn't one of them, they said. I was some kind of freak. My answer to them was always simple: "Basketball is what's going to keep me walking around here without pushing a stroller." I wasn't ashamed. I had no reason to be. And their attitude changed once I got into high school and everyone started talking about what a great player I had become, and what the future held for me. The *New York Post* and the *Daily News* and the *Times* all started writing about me, and the recruiters came calling, and everybody in the neighborhood knew who I was. Nobody messed with me. I was *Chamique*. I was going places, they said, and nobody wanted to screw that up. Deep down, they were proud.

The truth is, though, that if I'd ever started to screw up—get involved with drugs, or smoke, or get mixed up with the wrong people or the wrong guys—my grandmother would have killed me. I knew that. So I never did anything stupid. All I've ever wanted is to take care of my brother and make my grandmother proud. That's why I stayed at Tennessee for my senior year, even though everyone kept talking about how I could make so much money by jumping to the WNBA or the ABL. Sure, it was tempting, but I never took it seriously. How could I? People were saying that I was going to set a new standard in women's basketball, and they meant it all—contracts, endorsements, exposure, opportunity. They called me the Michael Jordan of women's basketball, which was flattering, if a little ridiculous. I was supposed to be the one to capitalize on all the great things other women players— players like Teresa Edwards and Cheryl Miller—had accomplished before me, and I was supposed to be the one to take it all to the next level. My game had arrived, they said, at exactly the right time.

To me that wasn't pressure, that was responsibility. So, what was I supposed to do when I got asked about turning pro early? Leave Tennessee early, get my shoe, get my endorsement deals, get my money, and forget about Coach Summitt and my teammates? I couldn't do that. That would be like taking things down a notch, accepting and setting a standard I didn't want others to settle for.

My grandmother always tells me that God gave me this gift, now use it to the best of your abilities. She tells me that I always have to remain humble. But she doesn't push me, ever. She says the reason why she doesn't say anything or bother me with too much is because I spent so much of my childhood being an adult, looking after my brother. The tough times my family went through made me have to be the mature one. Now she wants me to enjoy myself, be happy. She says I'm too serious. Maybe she's right. At times, I feel like I *need* to laugh. That's why I'll act silly with my friends, sometimes even in situations that don't seem all that funny. It's because I need to laugh so I can relax and cope with what's happening.

But you never get too far away from where you came from, that much I know. And I think that's a blessing. I think I can hang out anywhere. I have seen all walks of life. I can communicate with all different people—whether I'm talking with kids at a school in the city or doing one of the banquet speeches I always have to give these days. I know how to keep it real. I have hung out with millionaires and been in million-dollar homes, and I have been with people, in their houses, who don't have very much. I don't look at any of them any differently. I've learned you just treat people the way they treat you. I think that's one of the things for which I am most grateful. My life has taught me how to appreciate things.

I remember one of the first times I was in a millionaire's house. There was this guy, John Thornton, and he was a big booster for the university. He had this beautiful home, and he invited the team there. It was before my senior year, and I remember I was walking out of the house and he told me, "You want a house like this? You win another championship this year, and you can have a house like this. You'll be able to have anything you want." All I could think was, *Wow*.

I didn't want that house, though, as much as I wanted to make everyone proud. I didn't want to be a one-hit wonder, someone who saw her chance and took advantage, without giving any thought to what was right and what the consequences would be. I wanted to set an example, a good example. And everything just kind of fell into place. I believe it is because I had a plan. I didn't bank on anything, and I still don't. I had my own plan: I'm going to finish school, and if I can't play basketball, then I am going to law school. And if I can play basketball, I am going to do it right. I'm going to be someone others can look up to.

And you know, I was blessed. I waited, and like everyone said, I arrived right on time.

DAVON HOLDSCLAW ON CHAMIQUE

My first memory of my sister is her being older and me just following her around all day. I always wanted to be where Chamique was. Mostly, I followed her to the basketball courts. I'd watch her play, and play with the other little kids.

Chamique always took care of me. She had like a warrior instinct. She was mean, but she wasn't *that* mean. She just took it out on the basketball court. Sometimes she and her friends bullied me around. They always made me go to the ice-cream truck. But it was fun. We played basketball all day. We played other games too and just hung out together. We talked. We got into arguments, but nothing serious. Mostly we did a lot of brother-sister stuff. We have always been close.

It was hard when I went to live with my mother again and Chamique stayed with our grandmother. She's my sister and I loved her, but I had to go my way and she had to go hers. I understood her decision. And we still saw each other a lot. On the holidays she'd come over. We'd hang out and do that brother-sister thing. Just because we lived apart, it didn't mean we weren't still connected. We still had a bond.

If you ask me to describe her, the first thing I'll say is that Chamique is my role model. I admire the way she strived to be a basketball star. We came from nothing and now she's a basketball star. And she didn't change. She's still the same. It inspires me. For me, I want to own my own business. I'm not a basketball player like she is. But business management, I know I could do that. Chamique asks me all the time, "What do you want to do?" I told her I want to go to college, because she did and everyone in my family has. I want to know what it's all about.

I guess I'm still following Chamique around, sort of. "Little tagalong" is what she calls me. That's always going to be my name. I don't mind. Chamique's pretty cool to tag along behind.

18

Chapter 2

Chamique in first grade.

There are memories of my childhood that make me so happy. Barbecues and picnics with my parents and my grandmother and my cousins. My dad teasing me. My mom helping me with my homework, making me do it again and again until I got it right.

When I think about growing up in Jamaica, though, it's hard not to think about the fighting. The fighting, which always came after the drinking. My mom drank the most, though I think my dad had a problem too. I just remember hearing them scream at each other at night.

It's hard to explain my family. My mom is a very sensitive person. She's kind. My grandmother—her name is June—says she spoiled her as a child. She also says we're a lot alike. I don't know if I see that. I was born on August 9, 1977, in Flushing, Queens, and my mother was young when she had me—only nineteen. She got pregnant her senior year in high school. My grandmother made her finish anyway. She went to work for the city, in a human resources job. Raising me, she still seemed kind of young a lot of the time. I'd want something, and she'd want it too. It seemed like she was always copying me, and I was the kid. I gave her a hard time about that. Her feelings would get hurt really easily.

When it came to school, though, she gave me a lot of discipline when I was little. She was so strict about my penmanship. I'd come home from school, do my homework, and then she'd make me write the whole thing out all over again, if it was even a little bit sloppy or I'd gotten some food on the paper. She was really big on that.

My parents didn't get married, but they stayed together. And my brother, Davon, was born on September 5, 1980. A few years later, when I was maybe five, we moved into a high-rise building on 168th Street, around the corner from Jamaica Avenue and near Jamaica High School. It's the first home I remember. It was a two-bedroom apartment. Davon and I shared a room.

Davon, he was a momma's boy, and it was up to me to watch out for him. He was always attached to my hip, no matter where I went. I'd go with my friends to the pool, and Davon would follow. We'd go to the basketball court, and he'd come too. We'd go to the store, and Davon would be right behind me. My friends teased me about that all the time.

I was the tough one, even then. I always wanted to prove how tough I was. Davon and I, we'd lie down next to each other on the bed and I'd tell him to make a fist and punch me as hard as he could in the chest. And then I'd do it back. We'd just lie there, punch each other, and say, "Stay tough. Stay tough."

My friend Anthony Holmes—he's still one of my best friends today—used to go to summer camp with me, starting back when I was only six years old. Even before I lived there, Anthony lived in the same project as my grandmother, and we went to this little day camp in Astoria, where my aunt Anita was a counselor. He was a little kid—he's still short, only five feet four inches tall—and the other kids would pick on him. Anthony was always getting into fights, trying to defend himself, and I would interfere. I was much bigger than him, and rougher, and I'd fight anybody to protect him. To this day, Anthony teases me about how rough I can be. "You're the sweetest girl, Chamique," he says, "but you have a temper. You're a bully."

My other close friend from childhood, Cheron Scales, still has a scar I gave him from when we were little. He says I was a bully too.

I was chasing him that day—I always chased him—and we were going down the back stairs when he fell and cut his stomach. I was maybe eight, he was seven. He likes to show the scar to people, to talk about how I was so mean to him when he was just a little seven-year-old kid.

In some ways I was like most little kids. I liked to play games, joke around, watch movies. During the summer months I'd play tennis. I hadn't learned to play basketball yet. We had a baby-sitter then, her name was Miss Harvey. She'd pick me up from the bus after school and I'd stay at her house until my mom or dad came to get Davon and me. Miss Harvey had her daughter and her grandkids at the house too, and there was always something to do.

When I was in fourth and fifth grades, I used to love the library. It was my favorite place. We weren't allowed to go out and do too much stuff. The big Queens Borough Library was the best, because it was a grown-up–seeming hangout. I thought I was being slick, telling my baby-sitter that I was at the library, like I was studying or reading or something. Mostly, though, I was fooling around. I'd go there, and the library seemed huge, and I'd read magazines, be silly with my friends. Even then, though, it was like everybody in the neighborhood was keeping an eye on me. If somebody saw us being silly they'd tell Miss Harvey and she'd call my grandmother. Even then, before I lived with her, my grandmother was the one looking out for me.

My best friend then was Nicole Howell, who lived downstairs in the same building in Jamaica. We were big tomboys. We'd go everywhere on our bikes, play sports all day long. Nicole is the one who lived my childhood with me, saw all that craziness with my parents. Whenever I go back to my old neighborhood, I still visit her and her mom, whom I always called Miss Sharon. A lot of times, when things were bad, I'd just go downstairs to Miss Sharon's and hang out with Nicole. They always took me in.

Things were bad a lot of the time. Mostly, what I remember from back then is what it's like to be home and your parents are arguing, cursing at each other, yelling. And I'd have to listen to this. And I'd have to listen to my little brother in the next bed, crying. And what I always said to myself at those times was, *I can't cry.* I'd never let myself cry, because somebody had to be strong.

They'd almost never be drunk at the same time. For a long time, my mom would be drunk, and sometimes my dad would come pick us up from the baby-sitter's because she couldn't. And he'd get us some dinner. Then we'd go to bed, and my mom would come in late at night, when were supposed to be asleep, and they'd start arguing, and the two of us would just lie there in bed, hearing it.

I used to sit on the top of the radiator and look out the window, watching to see if my mother was going to come home, and if she was coming home, whether or not she'd be drunk. Most times she was, and I'd have to steal money out of her purse to go get food for Davon and me. Sometimes she wouldn't come home at all. Those times, I could never decide what to do. Did I take Davon with me to the store, even though he was only six or seven years old? Most times I'd leave him in the apartment, tell him to lock the door and only answer if somebody knocked twice and said my name, because that would be our secret password.

After a while, it almost becomes a routine. You depend on your dad to leave money for dinner, just in case your mom doesn't come home. You go out every day to find something to eat. You get takeout all the time—pizza, subs, sandwiches, things like that—bring it home to share with your brother. You can cook some things, hamburgers and stuff, but only if you have food at home. You learn to forge your mom's signature on your teacher reports and report cards because she's either too drunk to do it or not there at all. You learn to get your little brother dressed for school because if you don't, no one will. You stop expecting anyone to take care of you and you start taking care of yourself.

It wasn't me I was worried about anyway, it was Davon. He was so young, and the hardest part for me was watching what it did to him. He'd hear my dad yelling at my mom, or just trying to get my mom to sit down, calm down—she would just be so drunk and out of control—and Davon would start crying, "Mommy, Mommy, Mommy." It was so hard to listen to, and I didn't know what to do.

Once, instead of taking ten or twenty dollars from my mother's purse for food, I took fifty. I knew I'd get caught, but things had been so bad the night before and all I wanted to do was go to the Sunshine store out on Jamaica Avenue and get Davon a G.I. Joe. It's funny, thinking about it now, how kids figure things. I must have been about ten years old, and I was convinced that if I got Davon a G.I. Joe, somehow things wouldn't be so awful, he would be just like a normal kid. I left him in the apartment that day, locked the door, and reminded him about our special knock. And I got the G.I. Joe for him, and something for us to have for dinner.

The next day, Davon told on me. He told my mom I'd taken the fifty dollars. He'd always tell my mom anything. But I didn't even care.

If you look at our family, who is the strong one? It's me. It's always been me, from day one. And I don't think too many people know that. It's not something I really talk about. I think that's why my personality is the way it is, and why I handle things the way I do. It's the same thing with people saying to me, "You've had it so easy. You don't know what it's like to go without." Those people don't understand. They don't know me. It makes me want to laugh, or just get angry. I know what it's like to go without two parents. To be sent away to live somewhere else. To see your family fall apart.

My parents tried to hide some of the fighting from us, but when you're drunk, that's not an easy thing. My mother had it the worst. I remember the first time she went to rehab. It was that place in the city—Smithers Center—where Doc Gooden and Darryl Strawberry went when they had problems. She'd come over to my grandmother's apartment one day all drunk, and my uncle was there, my uncle Thurman, my mom's brother. He had come home for the summer. And he just grabbed my mother and took her to detox. He wasn't going to stand for any of it anymore.

We went to stay with my grandmother while my mom was in Smithers, because my dad was working so much. He came over every night, and spent the weekends with us too. I was so happy then, because I believed that this meant my mother was not going to drink anymore. I was just a young kid, and it was traumatizing to see my mother the way she was all the time. I was embarrassed. I didn't want her to be around me. More than anything, I wanted it to stop. And when she went to rehab, I believed it would.

We would go visit her and she seemed fine, and it gave me a lot of hope. I remember my mom standing outside talking to this other lady—a white lady, with black hair—and my mom was saying, "I am so happy to be getting out of here." I didn't like the lady, I don't know why, but I remember my mom's words registered and they seemed positive, positive to her recovery. "I'm happy to be out of here." That sounded good, right?

It was two days later when I saw my mom drinking again. Only two days after she got out. I remember it was pink champagne. Pink champagne, in one of those little bottles. I saw my mom with it in the living room and I stopped and said to her, "Mom, you're drinking?"

And she said, "It'll be all right."

She just kept saying that: "I'm going to be all right." Only she wasn't. I called my grandmother, and she started arguing with my mom, but it didn't make a difference. Pink champagne became a beer, and one beer led to the next, and my mom was getting drunk again. Just like that.

When I stop to let myself think about it—and I don't do that very often—I remember so much about when we were living in Jamaica. Showing up late for school because my mom would be hungover in the morning and she didn't get us up. Listening to Davon cry. Standing there, so many times, yelling furiously at my mother.

"Why are you doing this?" I'd scream. "Why?"

When my dad wasn't there, my mom would turn the radio up and be crazy, and Davon and I would be in our room, supposed to be asleep, and I'd start thinking, *I can't take this. I can't take this.* One night it was so bad that I took Davon out of bed, and we got dressed and got on the train and went to my grandmother's. It was late, and dark, and we had to take a train and then a bus to get to Astoria. I must have been ten then, and Davon was seven. I was holding on to Davon, telling him it was going to be okay. And then we got to my grandmother's apartment, safe. My grandmother was horrified. She kept saying, "This can't happen anymore."

My grandmother would try to talk to me about it. She'd tell me that people have different diseases, and that alcoholism happens to be the disease that my mother had. She tried to take me to meetings, Al-Anon, Alateen. I was ten then, and I didn't want any part of that. Miss Harvey tried to keep an eye on us too, but mostly she'd be calling my grandmother, telling her that we were left to run wild.

This is why my brother and I are so close—still to this day—and why I am so independent. I was taking care of both of us when I was nine years old. I took care of us for a few years, while I watched our family collapse.

Things got worse gradually. I would keep hearing my parents argue, and I'd always blame my mom, because my dad and I are closer. It was different for Davon, he was always closer to my mother. But they didn't fight over us. And they never hurt us. They just fought with each other, mostly about the drinking.

Eventually my mom just said my dad had to go. I was so hurt and so angry. I missed him so much. He only moved a few blocks away, so we could see each other. I'd get up in the morning and go downstairs, and he'd be outside waiting to take me to school. He'd give me money for school, and he'd call me after school, just to check in. He was worried about Davon and me and whether we had what we needed. He missed us, but my mom kept saying, "Your dad can't come here." I'd get so upset with her, and I started mouthing off to her, because I thought she was pushing him away.

She let him come back sometimes, though. He was there, I remember, the night Davon and I finally left to go live with my grandmother. It was one of those nights when I went downstairs to see Nicole. Davon was with me, as always. My dad had been drinking, I'm pretty sure. He was in the apartment by himself. I didn't have a key, so we were downstairs in Miss Sharon's house, hanging out with Nicole. My dad had been cooking, but he fell asleep, and things started burning, and there was all this smoke. I didn't know at first, I was downstairs and just decided it was time to go home. I told Nicole, "I'm going home," and Miss Sharon said good night.

The first time I went upstairs, I took Davon, and nobody

answered when we knocked, so we went back to Miss Sharon's. The second time, I went up alone, to check and see if my dad was home. I was banging on the door of the apartment and ringing the bell when one of my neighbors poked his head out the door and told me he was sure my dad was home because he'd heard him come in. It was like that where we lived, a little community, everybody knowing everybody else's business. If I came home and nobody answered at my house and I couldn't get in, I could always go stay at the neighbor's house or go stay with Miss Sharon.

The police came that night. Because of the smoke, or maybe because one of the neighbors called, I don't know. I just remember standing outside the door when they got there.

"I know my dad is in there," I told them.

So they started banging on the door and banging on the door, yelling for my father. The neighbors were coming out now, watching. Finally my dad answered. And when he opened the door there was all this smoke, and it smelled like everything was burning. The fire wasn't bad, but the situation was. The police wanted to take my dad down to the station to have a talk. They wanted us all to come—my dad, me, Davon. I started crying. I told them I had to call my grandmother.

We stayed at the police precinct most of that night. My mom eventually came home, and she was drunk, and that made things even worse. My grandmother had to come down to the station to get us. I was crying so much then. I was eleven years old and I was scared and I didn't know what was going to happen.

My grandmother was so angry when she got there. She came with my aunt Hattie. I was so young, I didn't know the logistics of it all, what was really going on. But I remember being told that Davon and I couldn't live with our parents anymore. There was a caseworker there, a lady named Miss Tioca. She told me that we couldn't live at home anymore, that my mother needed to go to rehab again, and that she couldn't have us back until she took care of things. And that's when we went to stay with my grandmother in Astoria.

Now that I'm older and I look back, I figure that this had to be an ongoing thing, that Children's Services had to be looking in on us for a while, and maybe a neighbor had called and said they'd heard what was going on in our house, over time. I don't know. I just remember so many days when I sat on the radiator, starving, watching and waiting for my mom to come home, hoping she wouldn't be drunk when she did. I remember listening to them fight and listening to Davon get so upset and thinking that I had to do whatever I could to take care of him.

When you're a little kid like that, I don't think you realize that things can be different. You just try to get through every day. And you try to escape, however you can. I used to ride the subway. I'd take the R train or the N train. I'd go to my grammar school, P.S. 95, and play with the kids at the playground. I'd go to different parks, swing on the swings, get back on, and ride to another stop. It seems kind of crazy now, a nine-year-old, ten-year-old girl on the subway with her friends, but that's what I did all the time.

My grandmother and I don't talk very much about what happened. What we do talk about is my relationship with my mother. For a long time, I was so bitter. I got even angrier when my mother started to get her life together and things started to fall apart for my dad. I don't even think I realized he had problems until I was older, when he started talking to himself and wound up having a nervous breakdown when I was in college. Clearly, he had his problems too. And they all contributed to what happened to my parents' relationship. But for years, I just blamed my mom. I just wanted to yell at her, "Why didn't you stop drinking? Why didn't you help my dad?"

I know she loved me, that both my parents love me. It was hard, though, to let all the anger go. In some ways, my mom is my number-one fan. In high school, she'd always want to come to my games, cheer for me. But I wouldn't let her come. I didn't want to see her or talk to her. I'd tell my grandmother, "If you bring her, I won't talk to you." I'd tell her again and again, "I don't want to see her. I don't want to see her." Seeing her the way she was, how she used to be, it made me so upset. I didn't want to deal with that. She kept trying to take an active role in my life, and I kept pushing her away. She'd come over to my grandmother's apartment, spend time around me, and I didn't know how to deal with it.

It took my mom a while to get into rehab again, and then she lived in a halfway house for a period of time, trying to get herself straight. It was about two years after we moved into my grandmother's apartment when she got her life together, when I was in ninth grade and Davon in sixth. She wanted us back after that, Davon and me, and I didn't want to go. My mom had gotten a place on Staten Island, and I was at Christ the King High School, and things were finally good for me. I needed structure, consistency, and I had that. I couldn't imagine letting it go.

It was just as hard, though, to let go of Davon. The minute my mother was allowed to have us back, Davon was ready to leave. I was still fighting with my mother about my situation when he moved out of Astoria and went to live on Staten Island with her. It was like losing your own shadow. All my life he was my little tagalong, and then he wasn't there anymore.

My mother didn't give up the fight easily. I remember her screaming at my grandmother, "These are my kids! I want my kids!" And the case manager told my grandmother that my mom was right, that she had the right to take us both back. But my grandmother knew how much I needed to stay where I was then. She'd argue with my mother, the caseworkers, everyone. She'd tell them that I was in a good environment, that I was in a good high school, doing well. That it would be too far for me to commute from Staten Island to Christ the King in Brooklyn, and that to move me now would be terrible.

It took a lot of work and a lot of talking—and the interference of some lawyers—before my mother agreed to sign over legal guardianship of me to my grandmother. It was almost a year after Davon had moved out before things got settled. Davon was hurt too, I think, that I didn't want to move out there, but staying with my grandmother was the best thing. I think even my mom knows that now.

My grandmother did everything she could to try to get me to be close to my mom again. She was the one who used to preach at me: "You have only one mother. I am not going to be here forever.

Learn to appreciate your mother. Believe me, you guys are going to need each other."

I think when I started looking at it in that light, that's when our relationship made a big change. It was about two or three years ago when I realized that I needed to fix things with my mother. We started to talk, to spend a little more time together. I started to see some things more from her perspective. She hadn't had a drink for more than five years at that point, which made a big difference to me. Addiction is a difficult thing to overcome, and I know my mom struggled. It takes a strong person to do what she's done, and I'm proud of her for that. I've also come to recognize that my dad had his own problems, and that I can't continue to blame everything that happened solely on my mom.

It's funny, when I was little, even after things got so bad, even when I was so angry at my mother, I always used to hope that my mom and dad would get back together. I think every kid hopes for that. But after a while you see that it's not going to happen. Now, I just enjoy both of them for who they are. My mom came down to see me a few times during my first season with the Mystics. She stayed with me, cooked for me, helped me find things for my town house. Things are finally good between us. We've come a long way.

Still, whenever I think about my family, I can't help but always wonder *why*. Why things happened the way they did. Why we all struggled so much. I think I need to know and understand, because it's where you come from that makes you. And a big part of me comes from the time when I lived with my mom and dad in that apartment building in Jamaica. It made me independent. It made me strong. It also made me grow up too quickly. And that was something that my grandmother did her best to try to fix.

JUNE HOLDSCLAW ON CHAMIQUE

Chamique has never really been a child—you know, like a little baby. Never. She was never really a little girl. Her mother tried to make her one. She'd buy Chamique all these pretty little dresses, but Chamique never wanted to wear them. She hated those little dresses. I think she wanted to be a little boy from the beginning.

The truth is, though, that Chamique never really got to be a child at all, which is one of the things I felt bad about when she came to live with me. Oh, that was a rough time. She was playing hooky from school and getting into trouble. She had a hard, hard time trying to adjust to my ways. She wasn't used to rules, and she was unhappy. She was used to being the little woman of the house. Before, she was running things, and then she came to Astoria and her whole life changed.

It was a lot of hard work, raising her and Davon. I was going to work, coming home, trying to keep track of an eleven-year-old and an eight-year-old, but it was far better than Chamique keeping track of them herself. Things just weren't going well in their lives then. I knew it would be best for them to be with me. I was more capable of giving them what they needed than their mother and father were at that time.

Chamique might not have had a mom and a dad right there with her, but she was around family. She had that. And her brother. I have four grandchildren—two live in Montana—and I love them all and talk to them all, but it's been different with Chamique, because we've been together so much. Sometimes I forget Chamique is my granddaughter and I call her my daughter. Her mom always corrects me then. "Ah, she's not your daughter," Bonita says. Chamique understands what I mean, though. Chamique knows that I'll always be there for her. There may be certain things I can't give her—like her mom and daddy, or material things—but I gave her everything I could.

Chapter 3

*Chamique, age eleven, flanked by her
grandmother (left) and her mother (right),
after her ballet recital at Lincoln Center.*

The first year I lived with my grandmother was my year of
drama. I was eleven years old. My parents were separated, my
mom was a mess, and now I was living with my grandmother in a
different neighborhood. I had to transfer schools in the middle of
the year, leave behind all my friends—including Nicole—and start
over. It wasn't easy. I was angry at my mother and missing my
father and wishing I lived with at least one of my parents.

I started skipping school a lot that year. I talked back to my
grandmother. I got into more and more fights. My behavior was
uncharacteristic, and now I know I was acting out because of all
the confusion and frustration inside of me. Then, though, I just
couldn't think straight. I started to reject things that had always
been important to me or had made me happy. Once a good student who'd liked school, I stopped caring about my classes. I loved
my grandmother but I treated her poorly. I was depressed, the
most depressed I'd ever been in my life, and I had no idea what to
do about it.

My grandmother could see it, and she did her best to try to help
me. She tried so many things—she talked to my guidance counselors, tried to get me into counseling. I wouldn't participate. I

knew what they were trying to do—I wasn't dumb—and I didn't want any part of it. I didn't feel comfortable talking about my problems to strangers, to people who didn't know about my family situation and what had happened with my parents. I think a lot of people feel that way. It's hard to open up to outsiders. Maybe it would have helped me, but I just couldn't do it. Not then.

It was a hard time all around. Davon was miserable because he missed our mom so much. I blew off everything, only went to school when I had tests. I still had some pride—I worked hard at those tests, managed to score better than passing grades—but I cut so much class the rest of the time, and missed so many homework assignments, that I was failing everything. My grandmother worked all day as a medical records clerk at Jamaica Hospital. She did everything she could to keep track of us, but I didn't make it easy.

I'd do all kinds of things when I was supposed to be in school: go to McDonald's, get on the train and ride around the way I used to in Jamaica, go into the city. I was aimless, something I've never been in my life before or since. The one thing I found that made me happy was basketball, and I played the game as often as I could.

My uncle Thurman was the one who first put a basketball in my hands. Thurman was my mother's brother, eight years younger, and had been raised by my grandmother in the same apartment where we now lived, until he left for college on a basketball scholarship. He was my grandmother's baby, and she adored him. I remember I was in Astoria when he first took me out to the courts, even though Davon and I were still living in Jamaica with our parents at the time. I must have been about eight or nine years old, and he was maybe twenty. Uncle Thurman picked me up on his shoulders, so I didn't have so far to throw the ball. I wish I could say I was a natural right away, and made a perfect basket, but I can't even remember. At the time, it didn't seem like a momentous thing. How was I supposed to know that I had just found something that was going to change my whole life?

I was really awkward when I first started playing. I didn't have a lot of skill or a lot of focus. I didn't focus on things very easily at that time. But I felt like I was always looking for something, some outlet, and that's how I fell into basketball. When I played, it was like everything was okay. Basketball became my shield, a way to protect myself from what was going on in my life. It still feels that way sometimes—it's still my comfort zone—but I don't *need* it the way I did then. Now, basketball is my passion. I love the game. But I don't depend on it to make me feel secure.

All the clothes I wore that first year with my grandmother were black. Black or really dark colors. My grandmother teased me about my wardrobe, but I'm sure there was worry beneath her words. I guess it was my way of expressing what I felt, of showing people that I was depressed, even if I didn't have the strength to tell them. Davon showed his frustration through his temper. He has a terrible temper sometimes, and I know that it comes from what he heard and saw when he was little. As hard as it was on me, I've always believed that it was harder on him. That he lived it more than any of us.

I was getting in fights all the time then. When you're from the projects, if a punch is thrown, you get into it. You don't back off. People picked fights with me, especially the other girls, because I played basketball. They'd tease me, call me a tomboy, ask me if I liked boys. They'd try to jump me. I always stood my ground. Besides, I wasn't trying to stay out of trouble anymore.

I got caught skipping school that spring, and it ended up being the best thing that could have happened to me. It was my job to go pick up Davon from his grammar school in the afternoon and walk him home. I was supposed to go there straight from my school, but I hadn't been going to my school, so I usually came from the basketball courts. Then one day Davon got sick, and his school called my grandmother to pick him up in the middle of the day. She came to my school afterward, to let me know that Davon was home with her and I didn't need to walk him. I wasn't there. The teachers told her I hadn't been there in seven or eight days. She was stunned, and she was furious. When I got home that after-noon, she sat me down and really talked to me for a long time. She talked about my bad attitude, my problems, how I needed to straighten myself out and remember what was important. She told me that if I gave up on school, I was giving up on my future.

By this time, the school administrators had decided that they were going to make me repeat sixth grade. My grandmother was really unhappy. She knew I wasn't stupid. I always scored very high on the standardized tests, and when I worked at it, I was one of the smarter kids in class. She didn't want me to have my entire education disrupted because outside issues were distracting me from being the good student she knew I could be.

I remember my grandmother going to plead my case to my guidance counselor. I was there, sitting outside the office, and I could hear them talk. My grandmother tried to explain that I was bright, but I was just having a hard time because things at home had been difficult that year.

I guess she didn't convince anyone, because the next thing I knew my grandmother was trying to get me admitted to private school. She sent me to Queens Lutheran, which was affiliated with the church we attended in my neighborhood. The school officials tested me when I first enrolled, and I tested so well that they put me back into my regular grade, and I never got held back after all.

After I started going to Queens Lutheran I had a total turnaround, and my grandmother had evidence of what she'd thought all along—that I was a good kid, but I needed structure and discipline in my life in order to excel. She was right. It's still true to this day. At Queens Lutheran I found that structure. It was a small school and the teachers were better able to watch over me than they had been in the crowded public school system. I liked that. Sometimes you need to know that someone is looking out for you, even if you want to pretend that you don't need anybody to take care of you. I'd gotten so used to pretending that I could take care of myself and take care of everyone around me—it was necessary to feel that way in Jamaica—that I'd forgotten how comforting it can be simply to be told what to do. To be told what is expected of you.

I even liked the fact that we had a uniform—a gray skirt with a white, pink, or blue oxford blouse. There was a kind of comfort in it too. My teachers were watching out for me, and so were the people from the church, and of course, my grandmother. My grades went back up. I started to remember how much I had liked to go to school. I made new friends, and we'd joke at recess and play around. I felt like a kid again.

That was one of the most important things my grandmother tried to do for me when I moved in with her in Astoria. She tried to give me back my childhood. Up until then, I'd only had glimpses of that. When I lived with my parents, there was such a burden on me. I thought I had to be the grown-up. There were times when we'd gone as a family to barbecues or parties, and I'd been able to laugh and run around with my cousins. But those times changed when my mother started getting drunk at all those parties, and fights would start. The only other time I remember really feeling relaxed and like a kid while with my parents was on our summer trips to South Carolina. For three or four summers in a row, we went to Mullins, where my father's family is from, and visited my great-grandmother Miss Lula and my great-grandfather and all kinds of cousins. It was country, that place. We'd walk around without shoes on, our feet crunching on the gravel. We'd even go to the store barefoot. It was real country. There was a field in the back, and a chicken coop. They grew tomatoes out front and watermelon alongside the house. It was so different from my world.

Even before I moved in with my grandmother, she could almost always tell when I was hurting, but once I lived with her, there was no hiding my pain. She could see what I'd lost. She said I talked with my eyes. That's one of the things that has always been special about our relationship. My grandmother can see inside of me, and when I was eleven years old, what she could see was how much I had lost or missed out on. She wanted to give all that back. She used to tease me, tell me that I never had to wash a dish in her house. It was her way of telling me that I didn't have to be responsible for everything anymore. That was her gift to me.

It's hard to put into words how special a person my grandmother is. Talking about it almost always makes me cry, whether I'm telling friends or standing in front of a thousand people in an auditorium, giving a speech. She's the most caring person I've ever known. She's the kind of person who treats everyone the same, no matter what, and I believe I've grown up to be nonjudgmental because of the example she set for me. She was tireless, or so it always seemed. She worked hard, but always remained patient and kindhearted. If I could be like anyone, I would be like my grandmother. There is no better example in my life.

I think it's her faith that impresses me almost more than anything else about my grandmother. It's unbelievable, it's so strong. She prays every morning. She goes to church every Sunday, sometimes more often. I remember her coming home from work exhausted some nights, ready to go to bed barely after 6 P.M., but then she'd be up at four or five in the morning, on her knees praying again. I'd get up to go to the bathroom, still the middle of the night to me, and there she'd be. I'd ask her, "Why so early?" and she'd answer, "This is my time of peace."

She always took me to church with her at Queens Lutheran, and to Sunday school. I'd chew gum and fidget and be uncomfortable, but it was important to my grandmother that I attend. The faith I have now comes from her, and those times. It took me a while to realize what role faith plays in my life, but I feel comfortable in my relationship with God now, comfortable enough that I have a clear view of what I believe and how I think I should live my life. And it's my grandmother who gave me that. She, more than anyone else, gave me the structure that has been the key to my ability to accomplish what I have so far in my life. My grandmother had rules, so many rules. I wasn't allowed to go outside when I came home from school. I'd have to call her at work, then stay inside until she got home. There were no more trips to the library to mess around, or aimless jaunts on the train. My grandmother knew better. She wanted to protect me.

Davon and I had a baby-sitter, Miss Jenny, who lived across the hall. I didn't like that, thought I was too old for a baby-sitter, but my grandmother insisted. She always told me that in a development like ours, there are a lot of young mothers, and they just let their kids run around wild. She wasn't going to allow that. I could never just hang out in someone else's apartment, unless my grandmother approved. I belonged to church youth groups. I had a curfew, 9 P.M., and I never broke it. I didn't dare.

One of the few places my grandmother let me go was the Boys and Girls Club, over at Twenty-first Street and Thirtieth Drive, about a ten-minute walk from my apartment. My grandmother liked it because they had organized activities, designed to keep us busy and away from trouble. I hated it because the activities were organized by gender. The boys played sports in the gym. The girls were supposed to do arts and crafts and other things like that.

I wasn't an arts and crafts kind of girl, that much was obvious. I'd get there, and roll my eyes, and tell Anthony and Cheron, "Man! I'm not coming here anymore. This is a joke!" I'd watch the boys in the gym, and already—I was eleven or twelve—I knew that's where I wanted to be. That's where I belonged: in the gym, playing ball.

Meanwhile, my grandmother tried to enroll me in anything and everything she could. For a while, I took ballet and jazz classes at Bernice Johnson Dance Studio in Queens. I've never been flexible, and I felt so awkward in my leotard, trying to stretch and bend in ways my tall, thin body just wasn't able. We used to have recitals, and I'd get dressed up in a tutu. There was one at Lincoln Center one day. I went straight from my cousin's baptism (I was so proud because Emmanuel Lewis—the little kid who played Webster on television—was my escort; he was friends with my cousin's family, and offered), but I got lost inside Lincoln Center and couldn't find my class for what seemed like forever. I missed our jazz performance—the only one I liked. But I still had to go out there in a blue-and-white tutu and perform a ballet. I remember being scared to death, and feeling terribly silly.

All the classes and organized activities were my grandmother's way of keeping me focused, and out of trouble. She worried about me all the time. She didn't believe in letting me hang out with my friends on the street, because she knew what that could lead to in our neighborhood. I understand it now, but when I was eleven years old, I was frustrated. She was overprotective, and there were so many things I couldn't do, so many places I couldn't go.

"If all you're going to do is hang out at someone else's house," she always said, "in that case, you might as well just stay at your own."

It took a while to adjust from the life I had lived in Jamaica, those days when I made my own decisions, and at first I hated that loss of control. My grandmother and I bickered a lot, often over silly things, but underneath, it was always affectionate. She was strict but she never hit me. She did everything by word, and I respected that. More than anything, she used to embarrass me. I'd be out on the basketball court past dinnertime and she'd hang out the window, yelling, "Chamique, upstairs!" All the guys would laugh and tease me. I'd go upstairs, like I was told, but I'd give my grandmother a hard time. "That's ghetto, Grandma," I'd tell her. "Don't act like that."

Anthony still teases me about the time I skipped church to play basketball, and I was on the court outside our building when my grandmother got home from services. She took one look at me, took off her shoe, and started chasing me around the court with it, screaming the whole time. The guys were laughing so hard they could hardly stand up. It was so unlike my grandmother to act that way, and Anthony can still make her laugh when he tells that story.

We'd fight about my room too, because my grandmother said it was always "a junk room, a mess." She was always telling me to clean it up. One time she took the door right off the hinges, thinking I'd be so embarrassed when we had company that I'd finally do something about it. But I didn't. I wasn't one for cleaning up all that much.

We also fought about the kind of sneakers I wanted. My grandma would try to buy old people sneaks, and I'd laugh so hard while we bickered in the store.

"I want these, Grandma," I'd say, pointing to the new Jordans.

"But those are a hundred and fifty dollars!" she'd argue. "You'll have to wear them for the rest of your life."

Usually, I'd win. I still knew how to get my way.

Despite all her rules, though, all my friends loved my grandmother and loved to come to our apartment. We'd tease and joke and she could always make them laugh. Cheron came over all the time. He'd laugh at how my grandmother would threaten me:

"I'm going to put you out, Chamique, if you keep acting like that. Stop playing with me!" I admit, I loved to make fun of her. Still do, because she takes it so well. I'm able to let down my guard with her in a way I can't with almost anyone else. For that same reason, I have an ease with the close friends who've watched me with my grandmother. Cheron, for instance, is like family, and has seen me at my best, and my worst. When we were in junior high, we'd go into my grandmother's room and watch television and he'd fall asleep on her bed with me. My grandmother never cared. She told me that Cheron could sleep over, because we'd been friends for so long she felt like he was one of her own. Of course, he'd hog the bed. I'd always be saying, "Cheron, *move over!*"

Of course, Davon was part of that world too. Growing up, Cheron and Anthony would tease me about how Davon was always tagging along with us, but they understood it. Whatever I did, Davon wanted to do. He'd come stand by the basketball courts and watch, or he'd come with us when we went shopping. Sometimes I'd complain about it.

"Davon," I'd tell him, "you're staying home this time. You can't be with me all the time."

But my grandmother always said the same thing. "Take your brother with you."

Davon and I, we would fight too, but it was that brother-sister kind of thing. All in good fun. Davon always knew I loved him, and he loved me back. Still, I'm not sure it was easier for him when we moved to my grandmother's, the way it was for me. He missed my mother so much and he didn't want to be away from her, so he was always rebelling. How do you explain to a kid who is eight years old, nine years old, that his mom is in rehab? How do you tell him that she has to clean herself up, then stay in a halfway house, and maybe—*maybe*—she'll be in a position to act like a mom again? He couldn't understand that. And he couldn't get why I seemed happier at my grandmother's than I had been before. It made him angry with me, I think.

Most people don't know this, but that anger is something that I understand, something I've shared. I do think Davon had a harder time than I did, but I certainly had my moments, though only my family knew it. Like I said, I'm different around my grand-mother. I can let myself go, and act out my feelings. Around other people I keep everything inside. That's why sometimes people think I'm arrogant, aloof—you know, a little distant, hard to fig-ure out. I'm an introvert, I know, and I'm trying to come out more, but it's hard for me. I just don't let people see what I'm feel-ing. I even kept things from my close friends. Growing up, not even Anthony truly understood how rough a time I had, because I didn't show him that side of me. I was too self-protective, too afraid to let the outside world in.

At home with my grandmother, though, there were times the frustration and rage would come pouring out. It would build up so much inside of me that I just couldn't control it anymore. And my grandmother understood. She'd tell me: "Not on the street, there are some things you should just keep inside your home." So I'd lose it with her. I'd really lose it. There were days when I'd tear up my room, tear up the whole apartment, just trying to let things out. I had so much anger inside—anger at my mother, and anger over what had happened to our family. I would rip the room apart. I would throw stuff. I would go crazy.

"No, no, I can't take this," I'd scream. I'd cry. I'd rip things from the walls, throw the covers off the bed. But I never showed that to anyone else. Like my grandmother told me, I kept it in the house.

That point hit home the other day when I was watching a movie with friends. I saw someone in the film lose control and tear up a room in frustration, and I couldn't help laughing. Out loud, to my friends, I said, "Why are they doing that? They're just going to have to clean it all back up!" I was laughing so hard.

Inside, though, I was remembering my own moments like that. My grandmother always made me clean up afterward. It was usu-ally my room I destroyed, and I had to fix it. But that was all she said. It was my rage, and she recognized that sometimes you need to feel rage, as long as you know how to direct it. Sometimes you need to get upset. That's why I know now that no one can push me to my limits, because I know where they are. I've pushed myself there—those times, in my grandmother's house.

My grandmother tried to give me everything. Everything. A safe home, love, security, structure, faith. And she tried to give me material, or expensive, things too—clothes, sneakers, money for my private school tuition, which got as high as $3,700 a year. I know my grandmother didn't make a whole lot of money—maybe $25,000 a year—but she always seemed to find a way. In that sense, I was raised by my whole family. My uncle George and aunt Anita were always doing things for me. We had a close family, actually, and one that was pretty generous. My dad tried to send money too, or bring me things. My dad and my grandmother kept a strong relationship, and he'd come by the apartment all the time to visit. My grandmother knew she couldn't give me back my parents—or at least the kind of two-parent family that all kids dream about—and she couldn't give me a big house or a car or things like that. But she always made sure I felt loved. She took care of me and she took care of Davon, even after he moved out and went back to live with my mother.

ANTHONY HOLMES ON CHAMIQUE

I've known Chamique since I was six years old and she was bigger than me, and beating up the boys who were trying to beat up on me. So nothing she does ever surprises me. It surprised a lot of people, though, when Chamique first started coming down to the basketball courts. We'd never had a female play basketball with us before. A lot of the guys were against it. But I'd always tell them, "You have to let her play because she's better than you." Chamique liked that.

Everybody knew Chamique. Maybe they didn't all approve of her at first, but they all knew her. As we got older, some of the guys started to get a little jealous and they would try to beat up on her, try to hurt her, do anything they could to get her off the court. It never worked. Chamique just took it as motivation.

It wasn't until after she'd gone to Tennessee that I looked back at the way Chamique's life had been and realized where she got that motivation. She never had it easy. She definitely didn't have an easy path to where she's gotten now. She overcame a lot of adversity, but she almost never showed that, not even to me. She hid it well. She acted like she never had a problem. She'd just get out there and play basketball, no matter what was going on in her life or what anybody had to say.

It's amazing to me, then, what she's accomplished. Astoria is still home for me. My grandmother lives there. My mother moved to an apartment building about two blocks away. So I'm back there all the time now. And what I see are all these females in Astoria who have grown up the same way Chamique did, and I see them having the heart to play sports just like Chamique did. Chamique is the one who set the path for all of them to follow. Without Chamique and what she has accomplished, I think those girls probably would have been afraid that they'd be teased—called tomboys, or told they must not like boys—just because they wanted to play ball. Now, none of them worry about that. They see how much Chamique is admired by the people in our neighborhood—people everywhere, really—and they just want to be like her. It makes me proud to be her friend.

Chapter 4

*Christ the King girls' championship basketball
team, with Chamique in the center (back).*

Uncle Thurman took charge of my basketball education from
the beginning, and I practiced with my friend Nicole in
Jamaica. I was only nine or ten at the time, and I wasn't strong at
all. I'd throw the ball underhand and look foolish. Slowly, though,
I started to learn how to dribble, and once I moved to my grandmother's and started playing on a regular basis, I got better and
better.

I never really minded failing. I just worked harder. When it got
cold in the late fall, most of the boys in my neighborhood left the
basketball courts and started to play football. I didn't want to be
left behind, so I tried to learn that game too. I wasn't very good, but
I was precocious—like anyone, I wanted to play quarterback. They
made me play receiver. I didn't let it discourage me. I was outside
all the time, practicing in the cold, trying to learn to run faster and
faster, because the boys were so much quicker than I was.

The boys beat on me when I played football. They tried to hit
me harder, and grab me, and do all kinds of inappropriate things
to drive me out of the game. I wouldn't back down. It took my
grandmother to put a stop to it. She watched what was going on
and pulled me out of the games. She didn't like what was happen-

ing. Still, I wanted to be out there. I loved taking hits, because I thought it proved I was tough.

I didn't tolerate it when people told me I couldn't do something or be something just because I was a girl. Not in my neighborhood, not anywhere. It only took a few weeks before the counselors at the Boys and Girls Club were letting me out of pottery classes and into the basketball games in the big gym. They didn't know how to stop me. I started out just playing one-on-one with Cheron or Anthony, but pretty soon I was in all the games. I was the only girl who played.

Once I started playing organized basketball, my athletic ability was pretty obvious. For one thing, I could grab the rim when I was only twelve years old. Most people my age—boys, even—weren't able to do that yet. I admit, I felt a little weird at the beginning, because I was the only one. I've never been much of a show-off. So if a lot of people were looking at me, I'd back down. My friends laughed at that. They'd say, "Chamique, grab it! Go ahead! Show them!" But that was just me. I was shy more than anything.

Astoria Houses is a pretty big place—maybe twenty buildings—and we had a lot of courts. I usually played on the center courts, which we called the middle park. My grandmother could see those courts out my bedroom window. Sometimes, though, Cheron or Anthony and I would go to the park near the water. We called it the back park. There was a lower rim there, for a weaker dunk. When no one else was watching except my good friends, I'd dunk on that rim. I was twelve years old, thirteen, and I was dunking. Cheron used to tease me, tell me it was because I was so tall. Anthony named those courts the "Dunkables."

To be honest, the game just kind of came to me. I guess when you play seven, eight hours a day, you're going to learn to play. New York City is the hot spot for street basketball. It was the in thing when I was a kid—at least, the in thing for guys. I'd sit outside my building and I'd watch the guys make these moves, and I'd dream about being able to play that way. I wanted to learn everything. I'd play three-on-three, I'd play one-on-one, I'd play all day. All day.

It was so much fun, and it kept us out of trouble. Anthony

would come knock on my door at 8 A.M. in the summer, and we'd go play, then I'd come back in the middle of the day to eat, take a shower. Then I'd go back out again. I'd send Davon with money for the ice-cream truck. We'd be out there until dark every day. Sometimes we'd stay out after dark, and play from midnight until 3 A.M., until my grandmother caught me and started yelling at me to get back inside. I was oblivious to the trouble around me. I was young and naive, my grandmother said. Looking back, I guess she was right.

Growing up in Astoria, everybody knew everybody. And when you're young, like I was, you have a different picture of the place. In the projects there are a lot of hardworking people, and a lot of not so hardworking people, and a lot of people who are just lazy. But then, I didn't know any better. When I was younger, living there was just *fun*.

There was this big area to play—all these basketball courts, all kinds of games going on. And we were on the water. People describe it as bleak, looking out at the East River, but I just thought of it like that: "We're on the water." There were always sports going on, especially basketball, and lots of kids around to play with.

As I got older and I started thinking about where I was going and the way my grandmother had taught me to live my life, I started to realize that not all the people around me had that same direction. Growing up there, you'd eventually see people you went to school with selling drugs, doing drugs, getting shot. It seemed so removed from the way I lived, even though it was the same neighborhood. All I did was play basketball. I stayed away from everything else.

The trouble never seemed to happen until it got dark, which is why my grandmother had her curfew and tried to keep me from being on the courts when it was late. Sometimes, in high school, I'd be up in my room studying and I'd hear gunshots. I'd look out my window and see the games breaking up, everybody running for safety. I'd think about how that wasn't cool. It disgusted me. But I never thought about it touching my life all that much.

I never got close to any of that trouble. I never even got offered drugs. I had people I hung around with sometimes—I call them associates rather than friends—who probably smoked weed. And some of the older guys on the courts, I knew they were smoking it too. I wasn't dumb. I knew what was going on. I could have done drugs if I wanted to. All I would have had to do was ask. But that wasn't what I wanted. And people never asked me.

I think that's why I was never really afraid in my neighborhood. Maybe a little bit, but not much. First, I was too young and naive to know well enough to be afraid. Then, as I got older, I had this special respect. Everybody knows one another there, like I said, and after a while everybody seemed to recognize that they shouldn't do anything stupid around me, because I had a future. I was going somewhere. No one wanted to do anything to stop that from happening.

That started to happen when I was in high school, and it's even more evident when I come home now. People in my neighborhood treat me like a little hometown hero, and I know they look at me and think, *She's straight, she's cool, we aren't going to mess with her.* These days, I could go outside at two o'clock in the morning and the guys on the corner doing whatever it is they're doing—and I know it's not good at that time of night—never say anything to me. Actually, they treat me well. They ask me, "What's up?" and if I ask them to carry my gym bag for me, or walk me to my building, they always do.

To a certain degree, though, I think people get too caught up in the rags-to-riches aspect of my story because I'm from the projects, and because of what that means about the environment in which I was raised. They don't understand that I enjoyed my childhood—at least in Astoria—because I had good friends and a grandmother who kept me out of trouble.

I learned a lot from my grandmother about having self-respect and self-confidence. Everyone wants to fit in sometimes, but I believe that you should never try to be something you're not. Be comfortable with who you are. When I was younger, I had friends who always wanted to fit in—fit in with this group, with that group. And to do that, they'd do stupid things, and I'd sit there and tell myself that I'm not going to do that, that people have to accept

46

me for who I am or they just aren't the kind of people I'd want for friends.

It's hard when you're younger, though. You just want to be with the in crowd. Only, the in crowd is not always the good crowd. It's the popular crowd, yes, but it's not the good one. And it's hard for kids to distinguish what's popular from what's right.

I struggled with that when the girls used to taunt me when I was younger, when they called me a tomboy and took away my basketball. It bothered me, but I never let it deter me. I knew what I wanted to do. They could take my basketball every day, and I was still going to play. I'd talk back to them, stand up for myself. I'd get into fights, even. But I wouldn't change who I was just to make them like me, or even leave me alone.

It's funny, playing ball with the boys wasn't cool—not at first— but I made it cool. I made it popular. And I made those people respect me. I go home now and those same girls who used to make fun of me, they come up to me and say things like, "How are you doing? Tell me what's going on in your life." They're proud of me too. As much as they used to make fun of me, they think it's great what I've done and where I am now. I see girls on the court in my neighborhood now, and no one is teasing them. Instead, everyone is watching, wondering who will be the next Chamique.

It hasn't been that long since I was getting teased as a tomboy— it was barely more than ten years ago—but I think it's incredible how things have changed when it comes to girls and sports. When I was growing up, girls weren't supposed to have muscles. If you had them, you were like a man. Now, muscles are cool, muscles are the thing. I love that. I love how people accept women as athletes, women with muscles, and that's what even guys want—for women to be fit, to be strong. It's so different. I remember watching guys look at a girl with muscles and insult her, tell her she "looks like a man." Now, they respect it. It's the cool thing, the in thing, and I think the success of women's sports has a lot to do with that.

Personally, I never really had body issues when I was younger. I was just embarrassed about having big feet. I was a gangly thing, always so thin and so tall, but I didn't dislike my body, or feel ugly or like I was some kind of freak. My feet were the only thing that could make me feel awkward or different. Now I couldn't care less, because I've grown into them, but I've had the same shoe size since I was five feet ten inches tall and in the eighth grade. It's the same shoe size Michael Jordan wears—thirteen. So imagine me then, in eighth grade, with these huge feet. I was so sensitive to that.

Another thing that bothered me was the way people would insult women by saying someone "plays like a girl." That phrase is so old school. They should just say, "She plays ball. She can ball." If someone taunts me like that—tells me I'm playing like a girl—I'm going to be more determined than ever to crush them on the court. I will make that person respect me. When I went to play pickup ball with the guys anywhere new, I'd always step on it the first few games. They might not play me hard at first, but pretty soon they're going to play me straight up, push me, do whatever it takes. Pretty soon all they'd be thinking was, *Okay, she can play. Let's play.*

It took a while, though, to earn that respect. When my grandmother first took me down to the after-school program at Astoria Houses and told the director, Tyrone Green, that I liked basketball, you could tell he was skeptical. None of the teams that played had girls on them. I was just twelve then, and he looked down at my feet, saw how huge they were, and figured he could give me a chance. He gave me a ball and I dribbled it for him. Dribbling wasn't even my strength then, but he said okay. He let me play.

The first time I played for that team—it was a PAL, or Police Athletic League, team—the boys moaned and groaned and complained. Anthony would defend me, tell everyone that I could play, they only had to give me a chance. They didn't like it.

By the next summer, though, it was hard for the guys to keep me off the team, because a lot of the time I was better than they were. We played in a tournament that year, the Mark "Action" Jackson Tournament in Astoria Park. My uncle Thurman coached my team—we were the house team from Astoria—and by then I had developed a lot more moves. In almost every game, I finished as the leading scorer. Pretty soon the guys had no choice but to respect me.

Still, some didn't. It was getting harder and harder to muscle me, and some guys resented that. They'd play me rougher than anyone else on the court. They were trying to hurt me, just to prove a point. They thought if they beat me up enough, I'd get off the court. I never did. I took it as motivation. Go ahead, foul me hard, I said. That will only make me stronger. If I learn to stand up to you, any hits I take playing against girls in high school won't even faze me. I'll be so strong.

For the next few years, I kept pushing. I played pickup ball everywhere—in my neighborhood, at the Boys and Girls Club, at another project, called Ravenswood. I played in a league with thirty-four teams at Ravenswood one summer. I was the only girl there. They'd ride me sometimes, tell me I stunk, tell me I couldn't play in their game. But I always got picked. People knew I could play.

When I wanted to be alone, I'd go to the back park to practice in peace. Out there, I'd practice my free throws, dunk, work on different things. I used to go out there even when it was raining, or when it was cold and the wind was blowing off the water. I always wanted to play.

Most of all, though, I liked to play in the middle park at Astoria Houses. I'd even stay out there at night and watch the older guys play tournaments. They'd play under the lights, and they'd string up a loudspeaker, have a DJ there to play music. I could have stayed out there all night. Sometimes I did. At least, until my grandmother stuck her head out the window in our apartment and hollered, "Chamique, upstairs!"

Tyrone Green was the one who told me that I needed to go to Christ the King, a Catholic high school in Queens. The school is really well known for having excellent athletics, but I didn't know much about it. I thought I'd go to public school. My grandmother had other ideas. She made me take the test to get admitted to St. John's Prep. She wanted to keep me in private school, no matter how much it cost. She didn't know much about Christ the King, either, when Tyrone brought up the subject.

I was thirteen then, and really athletic. I couldn't shoot with my left hand yet, but I could dribble, I could move. Tyrone had a reputation for helping guys in the neighborhood get into the right schools, and helping them get looked at by colleges, get scholarships. So when he said, "Chamique, you're going to Christ the King," I paid attention. My grandmother was harder to convince.

At the time, Christ the King was coached by Vinny Cannizzaro, a former cop who had become a mentor for some of the best female players in the city. He ran the Amateur Athletic Union, or AAU, teams for the girls in the summer, took them to camps, got college scholarships for so many of his players that the best college coaches were always calling him, looking to see who was coming up next. In New York, high school basketball is a big deal, and if you get with the right program, you get all kinds of exposure. You can travel with the big-name private high schools to play in tournaments around the country. You travel with your summer-league team, play at tournaments and camps. It's like a showcase for college scouts, and you pretty much want to get into the right program. So Tyrone was looking out for me.

He called Coach Cannizzaro one day in late May, when I was about to finish eighth grade. Tyrone had never called him before, because he'd never coached a girl before, but he knew enough to know that Coach Cannizzaro's program was the best.

"You've got to see this kid play," Tyrone told Coach Cannizzaro. "She wants to go to Christ the King."

Coach Cannizzaro said fine, whatever, and asked where we were playing that weekend. We were going to be down the street at P.S. 171 then, a grammar school. We had a practice scheduled. So Tyrone gave Coach Cannizzaro the information, and we expected him to come.

I was already on the court, working out, when Tyrone met Coach Cannizzaro around the corner and brought him into the park. He wasn't prepared to see a team of boys—he thought I'd be playing with girls. He had to look closely at first to recognize that I was out there at all.

We were doing a drill, one where a player would cut in, the coach would make the pass, and another player would rush on defense. I got my turn, flashed to the ball, made my cut, took it to the basket. I didn't even know I was being watched at the time. Coach Cannizzaro watched, said a few things to Tyrone, then just left.

Afterward, Tyrone told me what had happened.

"I asked him why he didn't want to stay and see you play," Tyrone told me. "He said he'd seen enough. He said he'd seen enough basketball in his life to know when he's seeing something special."

Coach Cannizzaro swears now that in that one short moment, when I elevated over the boys and took it to the hoop in one fluid motion, he'd seen something he hadn't seen from a girl before, let alone one who wasn't yet in ninth grade. He says he saw the future of the game. His mind was made up immediately.

Shortly after that, I went with my grandmother to visit the school. It was a long bus ride for me to Christ the King—it would take me twenty minutes more each way than it would to go to St. John's Prep, and I had to take a city bus—and my grandmother didn't really like that. She didn't understand about the basketball. She had no idea then what it could mean for me. I didn't really know all that well, either. I just know I liked the school when we went to visit. And I liked Coach Cannizzaro. He asked me how good I wanted to be. I told him the best. He liked that. And I meant it.

My grandmother was harder to convince. Tyrone couldn't persuade her. That's when my uncle Thurman stepped in. He knew basketball, and he sat my grandmother down and tried to explain that it would be looking out for my best interests to let me go play for Coach Cannizzaro.

"If Chamique is interested in basketball," Thurman said, "then Christ the King is one of the best high schools for basketball anywhere. And it's a good school. A Catholic school. They'll watch out for her."

As always, my grandmother respected Thurman's opinion. And Christ the King wasn't going to cost any more than she was already trying to scrape together for St. John's Prep. So she said okay.

Right away, Coach Cannizzaro made me a part of the family. I didn't know anything about AAU ball—organized basketball for girls. I'd never played on an organized girls' team, actually. All I'd ever done was play with the boys—on the PAL team, in the park leagues, on the courts in the projects. But even though the summer season had already started and I wouldn't be in high school until the fall, Coach Cannizzaro put me on a team with fourteen-year-olds he had been coaching. I was the youngest kid, the only one who hadn't already played in high school. It was a little overwhelming, but it was exciting too. We traveled so many places— Philadelphia, New Jersey, Boston, Connecticut. It was my first time out of the city, other than our family trips to South Carolina. Everything was new to me. I had never known there were girls' teams like this, or opportunities to play against so much competition.

I didn't know it then, but already I was getting exposure, the kind of exposure that prompts college programs to send you recruiting letters when you're not even finished with your freshman year of high school.

We went to the Eastern Invitational Basketball Camp that summer, at the College of New Jersey in Ewing. All the girls from Christ the King went there, and Coach Cannizzaro let me come, too. There were two divisions at the camp—one for the older girls, the juniors and seniors, and one for the younger girls, the ones in ninth and tenth grades. A lot of the Christ the King girls would get moved up to the older division because they were so good, and the coaches wanted to move me up too. But I didn't want to. I didn't want to play against girls that big. I was intimidated.

Even then, I was the youngest player in the younger division— everyone else had already started high school. But Coach Cannizzaro was so impressed by how well I was playing that he'd bring the college coaches over to watch me. "Look at her," he'd tell them. "She's dominating, and she's only thirteen." And the coaches, they were impressed.

I didn't know any of this then. I didn't realize what was going on around me, that a part of my future was starting to form, piece by piece, every time a college recruiter saw me pick up a basketball. To me it was just this amazing summer when I traveled to all these places and played with girls for the first time. I remember a tournament in Philadelphia, when I had what Coach Cannizzaro refers to as a Kodak moment. Usually at these kinds of tournaments the gyms are set up so that there are three courts going at the same time, side by side, and the coaches watch from the sidelines in between. Here, Coach Cannizzaro had to sit at the end of the court, under the basket, because of the way the courts were arranged.

The game was tough for me because I was younger and skinnier than most of the other girls. That didn't stop me, though. As Coach Cannizzaro tells it, I just kept flying down the lane, and at one point my teammate fed me the ball. I was so excited that I took off from about the foul line, soaring toward the basket. On the baseline, next to Coach Cannizzaro, two boys were running the score clocks. Their mouths dropped open as I flew toward them and dropped the ball in the hoop.

"Oh my God!" one of the boys said so loudly that Coach Cannizzaro couldn't help but hear.

The kid couldn't believe a girl had done that. I love that story. Love it when I get to show the boys a little something about what a girl can do.

COACH VINNY CANNIZZARO ON CHAMIQUE

There is no question that the word got around pretty quickly that we had this special young player at Christ the King. Everybody knew about Chamique before she even knew it herself. The college coaches and recruiters were interested before she even played her first game for me. They had just *heard* about her, from someone who had seen her play summer ball. It was obvious to anyone who knew anything about basketball that this was a special player. She was that good.

I think back on coaching her for four years, and Chamique created so many memorable moments. I remember one game in particular. It was her senior season, and our first game of the year. We were playing in Altoona, Pennsylvania, against a team that was ranked number four in the country. We had graduated a lot of players the year before, so we'd only been ranked number twelve or number fourteen or something like that. We had to prove ourselves.

The place was jam-packed, and Chamique was on fire from the beginning. She always liked to be aggressive. She hit her first twelve shots in a row that night. And I remember number eleven the best. She came down the court, went up in the air, elevating over everyone out there, and then she just did what was almost a 360, stuck the ball out, and put it in the basket. The place went crazy. And when she missed her thirteenth shot, the entire gym stood up and cheered for her, like they couldn't believe she was even human. On the radio, the announcers had run out of superlatives.

There was a reporter from the *New York Times* at the game that night, and he wrote an article about Chamique. In it, he talked about how this young girl was changing basketball. I don't think even he could have known then, though, how much of a change she would bring.

Chapter 5

Graduating from Christ the King.

I was nervous the first day I went to Christ the King. The bus ride was long—almost thirty minutes—and my grandmother came with me that day, just to make sure I was safe. When we came up the hill to the school, I could feel the butterflies in my stomach. It's a big place, with stained glass windows in the front and a cemetery that surrounds the campus. And though I'd seen it before, when I came for my visits, it seemed monstrous next to Queens Lutheran, my grammar school.

I was five feet ten inches tall then, and I only weighed about 122 pounds, and the coaches joked that my sneakers were bigger than I was. I was a puny thing, all legs in my gray uniform skirt, my arms long and skinny in my white oxford blouse with the blue vest. And I was shy, so shy. I had one friend from the projects, Rashard, a football player who lived in Queensbridge Houses and rode the bus with me every day. He'd played ball against me at Ravenswood in the summer. And like me, he'd come to Christ the King for athletics.

Most of my friends—almost all of them—had gone to St. John's Prep, and I knew almost no one at Christ the King those first few weeks. I'd get lost in the yellow-and-beige hallways, have trouble finding my classrooms. The place was huge. I used to go home to

Astoria and tell people, "Dag! My high school is like a college campus!" There were eighteen hundred kids at the school.

My freshman homeroom was in room 108B, and my homeroom teacher was Miss Carol Guerin. She taught me math my sophomore and junior years, and turned out to be my favorite teacher at Christ the King. She passed away in 1999. I was so sorry to hear that.

I was quiet in school, and almost never raised my hand in class, but I liked it there. I liked the fact that there was a lot of structure. Study halls, rules, that kind of thing. And with basketball, my days were full. I had almost no time to fool around.

When we first started practice, Coach Cannizzaro and his staff wondered if I could talk at all. I was that shy. Our team was ranked number two in the country, and I was the only freshman, and it was very intimidating at first. They thought about putting me on the junior varsity, especially since I hadn't filled out yet, as Assistant Coach Bob Mackey put it, but they decided I was ready to be on varsity anyway.

Still, I rarely played. We had so many good players that year, and Coach Cannizzaro didn't want to rush me or put too much pressure on me. He knew I had a lot of talent, he just wanted to make sure I developed at the right pace.

Practice could be torture for me, though, because the coaches used to match me up against Nakia Hill, a senior who was our captain. Nakia was so big she scared me—and she got angry a lot, too. A big girl with a temper, that was Nakia. She was six feet three inches tall and 220 pounds, and I was so scrawny I kept falling down. Sometimes I thought she was going to just crush me like a bug.

That was a confusing time for me, but I never questioned Coach Cannizzaro. I went to practice every day, did what I was told. We traveled to all these places, and the gyms were always packed to watch us play. One time, at a game in Ohio, there were more than five thousand people in the stands, and the overflow—maybe a thousand more—watched outside on a big-screen TV. It was incredible.

At home, my family came to the games, and after a while I was a little upset and embarrassed that I wasn't really playing. But I just kept playing with the guys in the neighborhood, working on my game, and going to face Nakia at practice. Eventually, I figured, I'd get my turn.

Coach Cannizzaro sometimes used me in the most surprising situations. We were playing a tournament at Christmastime against a team from Palos Verdes, California, that was ranked number one in the country—we were still number two—and I remember he called for me to sub, and I was stunned. I was so nervous that day that my hands were shaking when I laid them on the scorer's table to check in, and Coach Bob Oliva—he was the men's coach at Christ the King, but he was announcing that day—had to tell me to calm down. We lost that game. It was the only game we lost my freshman year.

My first and only start that season came in the Catholic League Championship. We were playing St. Peter's, and the game was played at St. Francis Prep in Queens.

The day before the game, two of my teammates—one of them Nakia, our starting center—didn't show up for practice. Actually, they showed up late, so late that practice had just ended. Coach Cannizzaro didn't say anything then, but we all knew he couldn't be happy.

The next day, we were in the locker room going over the lineups and our matchups and Coach Cannizzaro named four starters, then he looked at me and said, "Chamique, you're starting at center."

I was shocked. And scared. I couldn't believe he wasn't going to play our best player. But those were the rules: if you didn't practice, you didn't play. Still, I wasn't prepared to get a start, especially not in a game as big as this one. I just stared at him, my eyes wide. Then I told myself not to be scared, just to go out there and play.

We won the game, and I remember that I didn't play so badly. I scored 8 points, grabbed 9 rebounds, even blocked some shots. Afterward, I got interviewed by the newspapers for the first of what now seems like a million times. I kept telling the reporters that I was just a skinny kid out there, bouncing around, not sure what was going on. It was great, though.

That summer was a turning point for me as a player. I played AAU basketball again, and I thought I'd do what I had the previous summer—play with the older girls, the ones who were my teammates at Christ the King. But Coach Cannizzaro said no. He made me play with girls my own age that summer, in the fourteen-and-under division. I rebelled a little at first, but it was the best thing he could have done for me. Ever since I'd started playing organized basketball, I'd been playing against people who were bigger and stronger than I was—whether it was girls much older than me or boys my own age. Playing at my own level was a revelation. I could control games, even dominate them. It was something I needed to learn, to give me confidence. I couldn't see that then, but Coach Cannizzaro could. And his decision made me an entirely different player when I returned to school for my sophomore year.

It's amazing how fast things changed for me. I grew a few more inches over that summer, gained a few pounds. The other starters on our team that season were juniors, just one year ahead of me. Suddenly I'd gone from the end of the bench to the best player on the floor.

I had learned to relax and be comfortable around my teammates by then, and had made some good friends. It was different for me, being on a team made up of girls. I'd never had that experience before high school, and it opened up my eyes. It's amazing how strong and confident girls can become when they get an opportunity to play together and all work toward accomplishing the same goal. You learn things about one another, and about yourself.

I wanted to be a leader and have people look up to me, but I was also afraid that people would think I was getting an attitude or trying to show off because I was the best player on the team. I wanted everyone to know I thought of them as my equal, but I wanted to lead at the same time. I didn't know how.

There was a part of me then that still wanted to fit in more than anything. With our style of play, we never really had to go to one person to be successful, so it was easy for me to just blend. If we really needed a basket in a clutch situation, they almost always went to me. Still, I didn't try to take over games or act like I could score whenever I wanted, because I thought that meant I wasn't being humble. I knew I had this talent and I wanted to use it, but I didn't know how to do it right.

Coach Cannizzaro was the one who set me straight on that. He sat me down and talked to me one day.

"Chamique," he said, "you're a great basketball player. You're better than other players, and there are certain things that you can do on a basketball court that other people can't. You shouldn't hide that.

"Go out there and do what you're capable of doing," he told me, "and don't ever try to just fit in."

I told him I was afraid people wouldn't like me if I did that. He laughed at that, and promised me everyone would still like me anyway. Maybe it sounds silly that I needed to hear that from someone I trusted, but I did. I also needed to realize that being different is not always a bad thing, that it can be a good thing as well. That helped me figure out who I was, and who I wanted to be. Even now, my friends make fun of me, tell me, "You're different, Chamique," and they're not just talking about basketball. They say I'm old-fashioned. They're right. What I know, though, is that being old-fashioned may be different, but there's nothing wrong with that. I'm proud of the way I am.

My game grew my sophomore year too. I could handle the ball better, and I was smoother, more fluid. People commented on how graceful I was on the basketball court and how I made difficult shots look almost effortless. I'd read that about me in the paper: "Holdsclaw elevates over players and plays the game, almost effortlessly, in the air." I started to get recognized on the streets in New York, and even to acquire something of a national profile.

It helped that Christ the King was so well known. We made trips to Pennsylvania to play Cardinal O'Hara or Archbishop Carroll. We'd go to New Jersey and play Egg Harbor. Once a year—at Christmas break—we'd take a long road trip to play in a big tournament. We'd go to California to play Brea Olinda in Brea, or

Peninsula in Palos Verdes, or we'd go to Ohio to play Pickerington High School. We didn't just play the best teams in New York, we played the best teams in the country.

Our sophomore year, we went undefeated and were named *USA Today* team of the year. My junior year, I was asked to write a diary for both *USA Today* and the *New York Daily News*. It was silly stuff, mainly. For *USA Today*, I'd write about what I did every day, a sentence or two:

> Saturday, Jan. 15: We traveled to Connecticut in minus 23-degree weather. Boy, was it cold. We defeated Stamford Sacred Heart Academy, 76–28. I played well, with 24 points, 17 rebounds.
>
> Sunday, Jan. 16: Today was my day to rest. I stayed in bed and watched a couple of games on TV.
>
> Tuesday, Jan. 18: Tennessee Coach Pat Summitt watched practice. I was impressed. A lot of teachers were absent because of the weather and I only had three classes.

It was fun. I didn't think much about it, and I was surprised to hear, a few years later, that Zakiyah Modeste—who would become one of my best friends at Tennessee—had read every installment. She was growing up in Mount Vernon, New York, then, just north of the city, and her father was a basketball referee who knew about me. He used to make Zakiyah read my installments, and she told me later that following my attempts to choose a college program helped her figure out what she wanted as a track athlete.

Back then, though, it was just another installment in the newspaper to me. I was in the papers so much that I hardly noticed anymore. Anthony teased me about that, and he'd make fun of me when we went to the store and someone down the block would stop and ask me, "Aren't you Chamique?"

Some of my other friends started giving me a hard time, though, telling me that people were talking behind my back, saying I had a big head. "They say you think you're all that, Chamique," they told me. I just laughed at that. I didn't care. My friends—my real friends—knew me. And so did my teammates.

And I didn't have time for anything else. My whole life revolved around basketball, school, and my family. It was pretty simple. I liked it that way.

My grandmother stopped needing to structure my life for me once I went to high school, but she didn't stop watching over me. We practiced in two different shifts at Christ the King. Sometimes the boys would get the early practice, and we'd be there late—practice not starting until six-thirty or later. Other times we'd get the early practice, and I'd get home at a decent hour to do my homework.

On those days, my grandmother used to wait for me after work, and she'd cook dinner so we could eat together. That's when we talked about all kinds of things—school, my friends, my future, Davon, boys.

My grandmother was always the one to bring up the subject of boyfriends and sex, and it totally embarrassed me. She'd say I could have boyfriends, but I had to be careful. I'd giggle and blush because I wasn't even thinking about sex then. Please! I would have felt so guilty, sure that my grandmother would have been able to tell.

To be honest, I was scared too. More scared than anything. I had some friends who were what you call the fast girls. Everyone talked about them. That was not cool, not cool at all. I didn't want to be like that.

"Chamique," my grandmother would say, "don't get involved with boys at an early age."

And then we'd talk about the girl around the corner who was having a baby at sixteen. It was like that where I came from—when you talked about things like drugs or teenage pregnancy, you had real examples who were people you knew. There was a lot of that going on, young people having kids.

"Chamique," my grandmother would say, "you want to wait until you are married."

My example was always my mom and dad. I think that's all you need in life—one or two examples to learn from, to build on, to remind you of the consequences that come with certain choices. I didn't want it to be like that for me, the way it was with my parents. They loved each other, and they're still good friends now, but having kids too young wasn't the right thing for them.

When I make the decision to be with somebody, I have to be comfortable. I can't date someone if I can't see myself really being with that person on a long-term basis. And when it comes to sex, I think that if you get into that situation, it has to be a person you want to be with, and not just for the night. What happens if you get pregnant? You always have to think of that. You can't just be out there sleeping with anybody. It has to be someone you totally trust, someone you can see yourself with forever, someone you'd be willing to raise a child with.

I wasn't as oblivious to trouble as my grandmother believed. I'd see someone I knew get pregnant and I'd think, *I'm not going to do that!* I'd see seventeen-, fifteen-, thirteen-year-olds get pregnant, and it was shocking to me. I remember I talked to my father about it. "What are they thinking about?" I'd ask him. He'd tell me they weren't thinking. Which is probably the truth.

I know what I was thinking about: basketball, not boys. I didn't even have a boyfriend until college. Well, I had a boyfriend in fourth grade. He'd bring me candy every day to school, and my friends would say, "You know he likes you!" He'd kiss me on the cheek and run. When we'd play games, he'd always tag me first. Silly things like that. In high school, though, I barely paid attention. I had guy friends, but nothing serious.

In high school I'd go to dances and social events, but even then I wasn't really into it. I think maybe I went to two parties my whole high school career. I didn't fit in in those situations, but I didn't really care. My idea of a fun night out was a trip to Olive Garden with my teammate Kristeena Alexander, or shopping at the mall. I just kept it real.

I was in the popular crowd, because at Christ the King the basketball team was so big, and everyone knew me. I was shy, but once my friends got to know me, I'd never shut up. By senior year I still wasn't raising my hand in class all that often, but I got called down to the office a few times for talking too much in class. I was comfortable at Christ the King. I had my table in the cafeteria against the wall, my teammates, and my small group of friends. What more did I need?

There came a moment in my senior year when I realized exactly how strong my grandmother is. It was the spring, and my uncle Thurman was killed in a car accident.

I'll never forget the day it happened. It still makes me cry. I had an AAU basketball game, and when I got back to the gym at Christ the King, there was no one there to take me home. My uncle George was supposed to come get me. He didn't show up.

Coach Cannizzaro was there, and he waited with me for a while, then we called my house. No one answered at first. Then Coach Cannizzaro made another call, and when he came up to me after that, just from the look on his face I knew something was wrong.

"Oh my God," I said. "Not my grandmother. Please, not my grandmother. Please tell me it's not my grandmother."

I was so scared. When he told me it wasn't my grandmother, the first thing I thought of was Davon. I always worry that something is going to happen to Davon—that he'll be in the wrong place sometime. He told me it wasn't my brother either. But he didn't tell me what it was.

The whole drive to my house, so many things were going through my mind. I walked up the cement steps to the apartment and opened the door, and for some reason I remember that the big picture of Thurman my grandmother keeps in the living room caught my eye, just for a moment. But I didn't think much of it at the moment. I was looking for my grandmother.

My mom was there, waiting for me. She's the one who finally gave me the news.

"Your uncle Thurman, he's been in a bad car accident . . ."

Thurman lived in Montana then. He was married to Stacey, who was Native American, and they had two of the most beautiful little kids you've ever seen—Thurman Jr. and Kasala. Every time someone comes to my grandmother's apartment I show them the pictures of those kids, brag on them. Uncle Thurman had been on his way to officiate a basketball game with his best friend, Bobby. Bobby was driving. It was an SUV. Some gravel or something came down the mountain, and he lost control of the car. My uncle Thurman was wearing a seat belt but he died anyway, his neck broken. Bobby survived.

I've never seen my grandmother the way she was after she got the news. She was devastated, heartbroken, depressed. Thurman was her baby. She adored him and loved him so much you could see it in her eyes every time his name came up. And after he died, she used to cry, cry, cry. All the time, she was crying. It was the first time in my life she let me see something had hurt her, and it took almost two months before she seemed to be close to back to normal.

She found her strength in her prayer. She'd go to church, and she'd pray in the house, and she would try to be so strong. On her way home from work on the train, she'd think about how she had been blessed, really, because her son had died a strong and happy man with beautiful children; he hadn't been taken away by drugs or alcohol or a gunshot, like so many of the young men who grew up where we did.

"This was the right way for the Lord to take him," she said.

My voice still breaks when I try to talk about him. It means something truly special that he was the first person who put a basketball in my hand. They always called him the "real deal" in our neighborhood. He was a legend himself—played for Rice High School, Riverside Church. He coached in the projects sometimes, before he moved to Montana. And he had so much faith in me. He always told my grandmother, "Chamique's going to be better than me!" And when I got more college recruiting letters than he did, I teased him about it. He promised to come to my college games, and he said he'd buy me a car when I was a sophomore if I did well in school. I've always regretted the fact that he never saw me play at Tennessee.

I got my first recruiting letter my freshman year of high school. They sent the letters to school, and the coaching staff didn't show them to me right away. They were trying to shelter me for as long as they could.

But one of my teammates, Kristin Fraser, pulled me aside one day outside the office and told me, "Mique! You've got some mail in there." So we looked. There was this stack of letters, from places like Georgia Tech, Harvard, Stanford, North Carolina, St. John's. There were about twenty letters and I said to Kristin, "Oh my God! These places want me? I'm not even playing—I'm not doing anything—and they want me?"

By junior year the letters were coming to our apartment in stacks. Eventually, I was getting twenty, thirty letters a day, so many that the mailman couldn't even get them in the box. He had to come up to the door. If that doesn't focus you, what else will?

My friends were so excited for me. They kept telling me, "You can go anywhere you want. It's so cool!"

By then my grandmother realized I was going to get a college scholarship, and she was pleased and excited, but tried to keep me humble, and calm.

"Just take it one step at a time, Chamique," she told me. That was her advice. Then she made me promise I'd get an education, no matter what.

And the letters, they just kept coming. At one point no one could tell me I wasn't going to go to Auburn, because my grandmother was from Alabama and always talked about how she'd like to get back there someday. I wrote it in my book: "Auburn." I told my friends, "I promise you I'll go there."

I wasn't really that flippant about it, though. I did what my grandmother told me. I started checking things out—graduation rates, tradition, chances of winning a national championship. I started to call the schools and ask questions. I called Mickie DeMoss at Tennessee many, many times. We started to build a relationship. Most of what we talked about was simple stuff, kid stuff. I told her what I'd done that day. We talked about music, and I teased her that she was probably a country music fan. She tried to convince me that everyone in Tennessee wasn't country. She told me they'd take care of me down there. I felt comfortable talking to her.

I was focused at that point, really focused. My grandmother and Coach Cannizzaro told me that this was an important decision. They gave me a list of things to consider, and once I saw the light, I knew. I *knew*. My mind works like that. It shifts when I know what I have to do to get what I want, and then I immediately form a plan. And once I had that, I felt really good about myself and what was going to happen.

Eventually I made a shortlist, and the coaching staff at Christ the King made up a letter that they mailed to all the other schools—there were more than 150—thanking them for their interest but informing them that they hadn't made the cut. Then we sent a letter to my shortlist, which included Tennessee, Virginia, Connecticut, Penn State, and Purdue.

Tennessee wasn't really an early favorite, though I'd heard a lot about Coach Summitt. She'd come to watch me run at school one day. By NCAA rules, she wasn't allowed to talk to me at that point, so she sat in her car, and I could feel her eyes on me. We ran a mile, then did sprints. I never was much into running. We'd run through All Faith Cemetery, which surrounds the school, these long runs that we'd call Indian runs. We'd go to the beach in Rockaway, do five miles out there. I always hung in the middle of the pack, sometimes even dropped to the back, though I gave it an effort the day Coach Summitt was there.

I saw her at some AAU games too, but we never even made eye contact. And I know she came when we played the Catholic League Championship game my junior year. We were playing St. Peter's again—we always played St. Peter's in the championship, and we always won—and this time we were at St. Dominic's in Oyster Bay, on Long Island. Coach Summitt and Mickie DeMoss came up on a charter flight, rented a car, and came to the game.

We were so good that year that it was a romp early. I had 32 points when the game was still in the third quarter, our lead was huge, and then Coach Cannizzaro gestured to me, then pointed to one of my teammates on the bench and told her to sub.

"Chamique," he told me, "that's going to be it for the day."

I wasn't surprised. When we played the other Catholic school teams in the city, we dominated the games pretty often, and

Coach Cannizzaro always made me sit when it turned into a blowout. Sometimes I'd only play half a game, if that. It wasn't going to be any different this time, no matter who was in the stands.

So I sat on the bench for the last twelve minutes, with Coach Summitt there watching. Maybe I should have been disappointed or upset, or told Coach Cannizzaro that I wanted to try to set the scoring record, but I didn't really feel that way. I was just so excited that we were winning again, and winning big, and excited for my teammates. I was jumping up and down all over the place when we scored. I don't know what Coach Summitt thought of my performance that day, but a few months later, there she and Mickie were, climbing into the elevator in my building, coming for an official visit.

When I opened the door, I didn't know what to make of Coach Summitt. She was tall and she had on a suit, and her hair was done, and her nails were done, and she had bright red lipstick. Everything about her was so put together and so businesslike, except her Southern drawl stuck out a little, and I didn't know whether she looked country or just fake.

I sat on the couch in our tiny living room, where my grandmother keeps my trophies and all her pictures, and my grandmother sat next to me. I was glad Mickie was there too, because Mickie was the one I'd been calling on the phone for months, building a relationship. We talked a little bit about the program and what I could expect there, but mostly we just talked. It was nice to finally meet her face-to-face.

Mickie was the one who really thought Tennessee should recruit me. Coach Summitt always felt it was a long shot. She didn't think she'd be able to convince a girl from the projects in New York to come *live* in Tennessee, forget about play ball there. But Mickie pushed and Coach Summitt listened.

That afternoon in our apartment, I saw right away that Coach Summitt can be intimidating. She's a very intimidating lady, very businesslike. Her eyes can get to you. I could tell from the beginning that she was very well spoken and very strong. She talked about academics and graduation rates and the things she knew my grandmother thought were important. She'd judged right away that my grandmother and I had a special relationship and that I trusted her more than anyone, and I think she wanted to reassure my grandmother that I would be well taken care of at Tennessee, and that I would get my degree. And my grandmother liked her right away. Being from the South, my grandmother felt at home with their accents as well.

Coach Summitt never told me that day that I would start my freshman year, which is what pretty much all the coaches were telling me. She never promised me anything. But I remember very clearly that she told me she'd never seen a player at my position do the things I could do, and she said that I could be the best player ever to play for her at Tennessee. I knew about the players who had played there before, and that made an impression on me. At first I was thinking, *Dag! This lady is nuts!* But inside, I knew that if you have somebody who believes in you, you can do almost anything, and Coach Summitt really seemed to believe in me.

I was also impressed by how professional their presentation was. Some schools would come and they wouldn't have answers to all my questions, or wouldn't seem all that organized. Coach Summitt got there and it was *boom! boom! boom!* Everything was laid out for me. They even had a study hall schedule, and could tell my grandmother how much time would be set aside for me to work on my schoolwork in an organized setting.

I liked that. I needed to know that if I left my comfort zone here in Astoria and came to play at Tennessee, they were going to take care of me. I didn't want to fall through the cracks, and I knew enough about myself to know that I needed a disciplined system. Tennessee seemed to have that.

I took my first official visit to Penn State, and planned my second one for Tennessee. I also expected to go to Connecticut and Virginia, and I think most people thought those two schools were the front-runners. But after the visit to my apartment, Tennessee had started to creep ahead.

I still had my reservations, though, and I talked about them to

Mickie. I had this image of the South, that it was *Beverly Hillbillies* or something—no shoes, a bunch of cornfields. Too country for me. And Coach Summitt was right—I wasn't sure I could go from living in New York to living in a place like that.

I still remember getting off the plane in Knoxville—it was October of my senior year—and taking my first drive to the Tennessee campus. I didn't pay too much attention to what I saw outside the window, because I was nervous. I went to watch the team practice, and that's really all I wanted to do during my visit, be around the team. The people are the most important thing, I think. I met Kellie Jolly on that recruiting trip. She'd already committed to Tennessee, and we hit it off right away. By the time my visit was over, we were sitting around together talking about how many championships we were going to win there together. Our bond began that weekend, and it only got stronger the four years we played together. I think she was the first one I told that my mind was made up. I was going to Tennessee.

Maybe I should have taken more time to find out what the city was like, the restaurants, the rest of the students on campus, but I didn't. I didn't really get a view of what Knoxville is like. I got caught up in the team, and the program, and I liked it so much I made my decision right there, on the spot.

I knew it would make my grandmother happy. She liked Coach Summitt, and she liked the fact that she had a 100 percent graduation rate in her program. But I wanted to tease her a little. So when I came back, I said, "Grandma, I didn't like it. I think I'm going to go to Virginia."

She was upset.

"I love it, Chamique," she said. " I think you should think about this."

Then I started laughing, and she knew. I was going to be a Lady Vol. I never even bothered to visit the other schools.

PAT SUMMITT ON CHAMIQUE

I think as time went along I understood Chamique better and she understood me better. I remember her junior year, after the SEC Tournament, she sat down on the bus with me and said, "Coach Summitt, I just finished reading your book, and I finally understand you." And I remember laughing and saying I should have written it three years ago.

To motivate Chamique, you need to talk to her one-on-one. Tell her what you expect. If you're disappointed in her, you have to tell her why and talk it through. Now, in practice I wasn't always good about that, but in games I tried. She's always wanted to win. She's a competitor, a big-play person. She wants the responsibility.

You take her style of play and combine it with her success as a collegiate athlete, and that's why she's known as just "Chamique," or even just "Mique." That's why I go to games and these little kids watch her and they worship her. You ask, why her? Why not Cheryl Miller? Well, it's timing. There is more exposure now. The timing was right for Chamique. But you can't dismiss her style of play.

She's so graceful and fluid, she can hang in the air, she can get a shot at any time she wants one. Not many women have the ability to just pull up and shoot over people. She's the only one I've coached who could do that, until Michelle Snow came along. It's like Chamique can elevate above people. She keeps the ball up and she has the one-on-one skills now. Once she improved her ball-handling skills, she had this ability to stop on a dime, pull up, elevate, and shoot over people. Guys do that. Women have not done that quite like Chamique. It goes back to making it look easy. I watch Pete Sampras play tennis and at times I think, *That guy's not even sweating.* He just makes it look effortless. That's the way Chamique looks on a basketball court.

Chapter 6

Chamique playing for Tennessee.

My aunt Anita and my uncle George flew down with me to Knoxville when I showed up for my freshman year. We'd sent my stuff ahead, and it was there waiting for me. Everybody came to meet me—the coaches, Kellie Jolly and her family, my roommate, Kim Smallwood, and her mom. Kellie and I were suite mates. They like to put basketball players together.

We went to buy me a bike to ride around campus that first afternoon, because I didn't have a car. I didn't even have a driver's license. When you grow up in New York City, that's not something you do automatically when you turn sixteen or seventeen. We took the train, we took the bus.

That first night, we went bike riding—me, Misty Greene, who was going to be another one of my teammates, and Kim, my new roommate. We were tired. I was excited and tired at the same time. Everything seemed so new. I was nervous, too, thinking, *Who is going to be my family down here?*

It was overwhelming at first, as I think it is for most freshmen going to a new school in a new place. I had class, I had practice, I had homework. I was used to that kind of craziness from Christ the King, but there I'd had my comfort zone. I'd had my grand-

71

mother and I'd had my friends, especially Cheron and Anthony, and I could just relax and hang out with them. Now here I was on this big college campus and there was so much going on, but I wasn't the type of person to go to parties, to meet people like that. And Coach Summitt always told me: "You are represented by the people you hang around." So I was cautious about making new friends. How was I supposed to know who to trust?

This was the first time in my life I really encountered something that I now deal with all the time: how to know who really wants to be your friend and who just wants to be near you because you're Chamique Holdsclaw and everyone on campus or in town knows who you are. Because you're an athlete. Because you're kind of famous.

My good, good friends are still Cheron and Anthony and my high school teammate Kristeena Alexander—the people who knew me when I was growing up, the ones who really know me still. They always treated me like I was just one of the guys. To this day, they are the friends I know will always be real with me, treat me like nothing has changed. Cheron will tease me if I stop being even a little bit humble, will tell me, "Mique, you get an attitude, come talk to me and I'll straighten you right out." Cheron will take my cell phone right out of my hand and start dialing, and when I yell at him, he just laughs. "Mique," he says, "trust me."

You go to college—especially like I did, with a scholarship and all these expectations—and you have to be careful. You have to think about what a friend is, what that means. For me, it means someone who not only takes from you but is willing to give. I know if things got rough and I needed somebody, I could just pick up the phone and Cheron or Anthony would come to me, right away. And if they ever needed anything, even if Cheron called me today and told me he needed money for books for school, or anything like that, I'd send it to him. We've always looked out for one another. I can depend on that.

I got lucky, though, getting Kim for a roommate. She was a track athlete, and she was cool, laid-back. She was even more laid-back than I was. I was a little more outgoing, at least when I got around people I knew I could trust. But Kim and I, we had fun.

We'd go shopping, hang out. She and I became close, and I trusted her.

And it was my freshman year that I met Zakiyah—the track star who grew up in Mount Vernon. The fact that she was an athlete too and the fact that she was from New York gave us an immediate bond. Kim and I lived together freshman and sophomore year, and then I moved off campus to an apartment with Zakiyah for my last two years at Tennessee. Both of them are good friends, the kind of friends I can trust.

All that didn't come immediately, though. I've always been a little bit of a loner, and I was really that way my first fall in Tennessee. I was miserable, truly miserable. I almost quit and went home.

A lot of people look at my relationship with Coach Summitt now and they think it was a match made in heaven. That's hilarious. It's only become that way now because I've matured and I understand how much she considers me one of her own. She made that clear to me in a letter she wrote me this past Christmas. In it, she told me how proud she is of me. I was touched. Coach Summit saw something in me from the beginning that I didn't see in myself. Or maybe I did see it, but I didn't know all the work that had to be put in to make it happen. It took time for me to understand that.

Our relationship could get pretty ugly in the beginning. Coach Summitt challenged me and I just didn't understand her methods. I didn't understand what she wanted from me, and when I don't feel like I know what's expected of me, I tend to get frustrated and lose my focus. That's what happened to me freshman year.

At first, when we had conditioning at 6 A.M., two times a week, it was tiring but fun. I liked getting to know my teammates. I thought I was ready for everything. I bought a little planner, because one thing about playing for Coach Summitt—you had to be organized. You had to keep a schedule, remember all the meetings, because you can't ever be late. She's very disciplined.

I didn't know how disciplined until we started practice. Then it felt like I could do nothing right. All day, every day, I'd hear her yelling, "Chamique! Chamique! Chamique!" It was like I was the only one out there. I'd be thinking to myself, *Dag! There are ten or eleven other people on this team. I can't be the one doing* everything *wrong.*

But on it went, day after day after day.

"Holdsclaw! Are you going to rebound?"

"Holdsclaw! Play some defense!"

"Chamique! Chamique! Chamique!"

The frustration inside me built and built and built until I felt I couldn't take it anymore. I felt like I couldn't talk to anyone on the team about it, because all my teammates had their own issues. But I didn't know how to handle it. Here you are, you're eighteen years old, you want to be good, you want to be the best, and this lady is telling you she wants to make you the best, but all she does is yell at you. Every single day. Every day—"Chamique! Chamique! Chamique!"— until you feel like she's put so much on your shoulders that you're going to break.

I'd go back to my room after practice and try to do my homework, then I'd lie in my bed, crying in the dark, trying to make sure that Kim didn't hear me. And the next day, I'd be up at Stokely, the athletic building, for individual workouts and it would be so hot, so hot up there all the time, and she'd be yelling at me again.

At first it kind of shocked me. Then I got used to it, a little. But there were still so many days when I felt like the only person Coach Summitt saw on that court was me.

"Chamique doesn't want to box out today!"

"Chamique doesn't want to play hard!"

Sometimes we'd sit in the locker room afterward and my teammates would joke about it, try to make me feel better. They'd say, "Man, you know it's your day when Pat's going 'Chamique!' every ten seconds." Everybody else called her Pat, but I called her Coach Summitt. It was the way I was raised. We would laugh about it those days in the locker room. That was cool. It was like stress relief. But there'd still be those nights, lights out, quiet tears coming down my face. I'd be thinking, *I can't take it. I can't take it. I can't take it.* Over and over and over again.

The days after those nights, I'd be bitter. I'd come to practice with a chip on my shoulder. Mickie would see it. She tried to talk to me, keep me calm. She thought I needed to be better organized, that one of the reasons I was letting Coach Summitt get to me so badly was because everything else was building up in my life. School pressures, homework, missing my family. But it always seemed like the things that Coach Summitt said to me were the things that pushed me to the breaking point. I'd go to Mickie so upset and tell her I was going to quit, I was going home. She'd tell me to calm down, relax, and I'd just yell back at her: "You always tell me to calm down! Do *not* tell me to calm down!"

Mickie was right that it was about more than basketball. I was lonely. I missed my friends, the people I'd known for ten years. I missed hanging around at the Boys and Girls Club. I missed my family—my grandmother, Davon, my parents.

Still, I was determined to be independent. I guess in a sense I've always been very, very independent. So I'd sit in my room and try to analyze things in my head. I'm one of those people who plays things over and over in her head, trying to sort them out. You almost never see frustration on my face, because I always keep it locked inside. Off the court, my teammates would always look at me and say, "Chamique, you're in the zone."

Other than Mickie, I didn't talk to anyone about what was going on. Kim didn't know, even though she was my roommate. None of my teammates knew. I'm not somebody who lets people in like that. I didn't even call my grandmother. I talked to her, maybe twice a week, but I didn't bother her with things like that. I'd only tell her afterward, when I sorted through things and knew what I had to do.

It was right before Christmas, and I had decided I couldn't take it anymore, when Coach Summitt finally sat down and talked to me one-on-one. We had played a game in Chicago, at DePaul. For days I had been telling Mickie that I wanted to leave, or transfer, and that I was serious this time. She told Coach Summitt, but they didn't really panic. Coach Summitt had called my grandmother, warned her that I might call, threatening to transfer.

On our flight back from Chicago, Coach Summitt called me up

to sit with her on the plane. It was an eye-opening conversation for me. She finally gave me some positive feedback, telling me that she thought I was making progress on the court. She told me she pushed me so hard because she wanted me to be the best, and she thought I had that ability. She told me she'd never push me to do something she didn't know I was capable of doing. "Just believe in me," she said. "And I'll believe in you."

Things weren't perfect after that, but they were better. We had another big blowout in February, after we lost to Ole Miss for our fourth defeat of the season. In the locker room I was joking around with my teammate Tiffani Johnson, and Mickie came back and started to scream at us. "You think this is funny!" she yelled. "If I were y'all, I wouldn't be joking around!"

I lost it then. What they couldn't understand was that I handled adversity by pushing it inside, and sometimes my giggles were just a way to release the pressure and the tension. And if they weren't going to take the time to learn that about me, and understand it, I didn't want to play for them anymore. I was sick of being told, "You need to grow up, Chamique!"

We had a terrible flight back to Knoxville, and when we got back to our rooms, two of my teammates started joking on me about what had happened. "You have three more years of this, Chamique," they told me. "Three more years." It sounded like forever. Once again, I thought about leaving.

Once again, Coach Summitt and I had a talk to try to clarify things. We could almost always talk things out, and I think that's when Coach Summitt started to realize that what I needed was to be talked to one-on-one. Yelling at me in front of everyone was not going to get me motivated, it was only going to make me more upset. She also started to understand that I dealt with pressure in different ways. My giggles, I told her, were not disrespectful. We just needed to communicate more, that's all.

The more she learned about me, though, the more Coach Summitt knew how to push my buttons, and she pushed them, again and again and again, in my four years at Tennessee. Sometimes she made me furious. Sometimes she made me cry. Almost all the time, though, she made me play my best.

* * *

It wasn't just my rocky relationship with Coach Summitt that had me miserable my freshman year. Moving to Knoxville was more of a culture shock than I had expected. This was a whole new world for me, one that seemed pretty bland and so much less exciting than living in New York City. I was used to living amongst people of all ethnic groups, and there in Knoxville, you were either black or white. There wasn't much cultural diversity. Even little things—like the food—would drive me crazy. I'd want Chinese food, and it wasn't the same as it was in New York. I'd want Jamaican food and they wouldn't have it at all. Tennessee was just totally different, and I had to make do with what I had. I was used to seeing so much, and that was just gone. Bam! Just like that!

Everyone on campus seemed to dress alike, look alike. You had two malls there—really only one good one—and you saw that in the things people would wear. I was used to going into the city, to SoHo, to the little shops. I loved that, seeing the different people, the different things, the different looks. In Tennessee, I felt like it was so small, you saw the same people and the same things every single day.

There were silly little things that annoyed me, too. Zakiyah used to complain that there were no little corner stores with the twenty-five-cent bags of potato chips like you had on every block in New York. I hated that some movies I wanted to see—like a little indie film called *Delicatessen*—never came to theaters in Tennessee. I couldn't even get it on videocassette, I had to wait until I was back home. Tennessee was just so slow.

To be honest, I never really got used to it. I just came to understand that I wasn't in Tennessee for the social life. The Lord sent me there to play basketball and get an education. I had my good friends, and I just needed to try and enjoy the situation, and appreciate what I did have. Sure, I had those days when I would think, *There's nothing to do. I can't stand this place. I can't wait until I graduate.* Of course I did. But then I'd think about what it was like when they toss the ball up in Thompson-Boling Arena and there are ten thousand people screaming for you, and how great that felt. And I'd think about how I was at a school where the coaching staff cared as much—more—about academics as they did athletics. Those two things together gave me comfort. They took away my frustrations when I needed it most.

The race issue was more complicated. I've never been one to think about race too much, but at Tennessee it was very different from what I was used to. My friends were pretty much mixed in high school. Kristeena and I were the only two black girls on the team at Christ the King for a while, but I would hang out with the other girls too, with Erin Fahy, with Jamie Buttner. And when I got to Tennessee, Kim and Zakiyah were black, but Kellie was my best friend on the team and she was from Sparta, Tennessee, and had a Southern accent and everything. We were definitely from different worlds, but it didn't matter that much.

The church my grandmother took me to growing up was more than 90 percent white. There were maybe two black families in the congregation. And the feeling I always got there was that they accepted you for who you were. People are people. That's definitely the way my grandmother raised me. She didn't keep me around only black kids, because she said the world wasn't made up of only black kids and I needed to be exposed to what the world is really like. Even in my own family, we have two interracial relationships—my uncle Thurman's wife is Native American and the kids are mixed, and my cousin Elon is married to a Filipino woman, and their kids are mixed. So I'm used to it.

Maybe I'm just lucky, but I've never been called the N-word. Never. But I've thought a lot about what I would do if someone said that to me. In the 'hood, a lot of blacks say it to one another. It's common to hear, "What's up, nigger, what's up?" on the street. If I heard one of my friends using that term, though, I'd always ask them why. Don't you know that that term is just ignorant? Why would you want to use it to one another when you know the minute a person not of your race calls you that, you're going to get upset? My friends know that's how I feel, so they never say it around me anymore.

Sometimes it seems like that term doesn't have anything to do with race anymore, because I hear all kinds of kids using it on the street to talk to one another—white kids, Asians, whatever. They call one another that, and they don't see it for the insult that it always was in the past. I just don't like the word said around me. It hurts people. That's all I need to know.

I wondered, when I got to Tennessee, if things were going to be different. I learned quickly, being at a college that is only about 3 percent minority, that people are going to treat you the way they are going to treat you. I felt most people were accepting. Certainly, at first, I didn't feel any racism directed at me. But the more I talked about it to my other black friends, the more I wondered if it was because people really were so accepting or if it was because they were just accepting of me because I was Chamique Holdsclaw, scholarship athlete.

Zakiyah always had stories about how she or her friends had encountered racism, whether it was subtle or pretty obvious. I heard people complain about the cops. And Zakiyah was right in some ways. People would treat me differently than they would other blacks because I was a popular athlete. I'd catch them at it sometimes. I would go to a store and a lady would be acting like she had this attitude, and someone nearby would say, "Oh! That's Chamique!" and all of a sudden her attitude changed. All of a sudden I was someone to be treated with respect. I hated that. I hated it when they treated me different than they treated one of my friends who is black but didn't play sports.

For the most part, though, I have to say the people of Tennessee were incredible to me. If they were behind me, they were behind me 100 percent. People in the program, our supporters, they always wanted to help you out, do things for you, make your transition easier. They cheered for you and backed you up, no matter the situation. And that made me feel good. It helps when people really care about you, and you feel like you have a family. I felt like I had a family there.

I had a little cushion when I arrived at Tennessee because we had two top seniors—Michelle Marciniak and Latina Davis—and even though the newspapers were talking about how good I could be and what an impact I could have, I wasn't expected to carry the team. Coach Summitt tried to protect me, too, I think. She told people not to push, to let me grow.

Coach Summitt was the only one who was allowed to push me. And she pushed on every level. My grades would be decent, and she'd send me to study hall anyway. It wasn't enough for me to do okay in school, I had to excel.

"Chamique," she'd tell me, "there are certain people from whom I expect certain things. You are one of those people. You are a good student, and you come from a good high school program. I'm not going to let you sit and just do enough to get by. You have to push."

She waited, though, to see when I'd be ready to really step it up on the court in a game. She wanted to see when I thought I was ready. Some people will say that I first really stepped up against Purdue, in early December, when I scored 27 points to lead the team. Coach Summitt definitely thought that was a big moment for me. But I still wasn't feeling totally comfortable.

A month later, in early January, we lost a huge game to Connecticut at home—it was our first loss in our home arena in seventy games, dating back to 1991. Afterward, Coach Summitt made all of us sit down and write our thoughts out on paper. I wrote that I had sat back and waited for the upperclassmen to step up and want the ball during the game. I had thought about stepping up, but I hadn't. I had waited for someone else, someone older. I wrote that I wasn't going to let that happen the next time. "Coach Summitt," I wrote, "next time, I'll step up. I want the ball."

There was an ice storm that day. We were supposed to fly out to Georgia and we were delayed, and Coach Summitt read our notes. And things changed a little after that. I got more aggressive, and she encouraged it.

Two weeks later, I made my big move. We were playing Vanderbilt and we were down, and I had this feeling that they couldn't guard me. I wanted the ball. So I went up to Coach Summitt, actually tugged on her blazer, and told her, "Get me the ball!" My voice almost sounded angry. "Get me the ball," I said, "and I'll go to work." I think that day was when I really first felt this deep competitiveness inside me, a desire to succeed that canceled out any fear of failing. I just wanted to give it my all, with no fear. I scored 18 points and had 12 rebounds that night, and we ended up winning the game by 3. That was definitely a turning point for me.

Soon I was taking the ball right from the start of the game. I'd almost always be on the attack, take the first shot. That was an adjustment for Coach Summitt, who always used to tell us, "Patience, patience. Work the ball. Work it." I didn't listen. As soon as I got my hands on the ball, I wanted to attack, make things happen. I believe that when you're on a team and you are the go-to player, you need to come out with an aggressive attitude and show your opponent from the very beginning that you're going to take it to them. You have to be aggressive, but under control about it. I call it being a "quiet assassin." That opens up so many things for your teammates.

This was the attitude I took: I wanted to put people on their heels. I wanted them thinking, *Man, this kid came to play. She's all about business tonight.* I wanted them to think that, and then immediately focus all their attention on me. If you do that, your team is going to find itself with so many other options right away. After a while, Coach Summitt gave me the green light—within reason— and I took advantage of it.

People ask me when it became "my team" at Tennessee, and I don't really know how to answer that. In high school, college, even now as a pro, I've never cared whose team it is—if it's my team or some other player's team—but there has to be somebody who is willing to take a chance. And I am willing to take a chance anytime now. Eight seconds left and you want to give me the ball? Great. I'll take the shot. You need me to make a defensive stop and guard their best player? Let me at it. Some people are scared in those types of situations and some people excel. I am just not scared. I was hesitant at the beginning of freshman year, but never again.

If I fail, I always think, well, okay, at least I tried. At least I had the guts to try. I have missed game-winning shots, and I'm okay with that. I have been in games when I've been the decoy in the last few seconds, and the whole defense is run to me because they think I'm going to take the shot—and somebody else scores the winning basket. And in those moments I'm like, "Yes!" because I didn't have to score the winning basket, I just needed to *win*.

I've come a long way from when Coach Cannizzaro had to sit me down as a sophomore in high school and tell me that I shouldn't be afraid to show people what I can do. Now, I know that God has blessed me with talent and I am not going to sit there and hold back my talent or what I can do for anybody or any reason. If I do, I feel like I'm cheating myself of my God-given ability. Whenever I know what my job is, I'm going to do it, and I'm going to do it to the best of my ability. And that is how I compete against myself. Because sometimes you have to compete against yourself. Sometimes only you can bring out the best in yourself.

And sometimes it takes a coach like Coach Summitt to make you realize that you can do even more than you imagined.

At the end of my freshman year, I sprained my medial collateral ligament in my right knee in the Southeastern Conference championship game. When I went down, I couldn't even move my leg. It was frightening. I felt helpless. All I was thinking was, *Oh my God! What happened?* My grandmother was there, and they took me back to the locker room, then eventually I made it back out to watch my team beat Alabama to win the title. But I knew I had been hurt pretty badly.

Everybody was freaked, and in the papers they started to say that our chances in the NCAA Tournament had been hurt because I wasn't going to be able to play, and if I did play eventually, I'd never be 100 percent. Then again, everybody had been writing off our national championship chances since early February, when we lost that game to Mississippi. My injury, they said, only made it even more of an outside shot.

I was so upset, because I wanted to play so badly, but I was hurting, and the tournament started in less than two weeks. I couldn't imagine that I would be ready to play. My knee was a mess.

The team had a meeting, and the players told me, "Mique, we're behind you." And Michelle Marciniak said some really great things to me about how the older players weren't frustrated or jealous or any of that because I was getting so much attention. She told me they were proud of me, and felt I deserved it. I was leading scorer on the team, even that first season, but I always felt that so much of the credit should go to the seniors. It was amazing, though, when they showed me support like that. Michelle even wrote me a letter after she graduated, thanking me for letting her "ride my coattails to a title." I still have that letter. It touched me more than I can say.

That spring, though, I felt isolated. I knew I had to work really hard, because I wasn't in my comfort zone. Coach Summitt kept getting on me, but I tried to close myself off and focus on what I had to do. I worked hard on my rehab, then went back to my room, studied, stayed in.

I didn't think I was ready to play in the first game. But the day before, Coach Summitt called me into her office and told me, point-blank, that if I didn't play in the first round, she wouldn't let me play in the tournament at all.

"Holdsclaw," she said, "are you going to do this? Or are you going to be a baby?"

I couldn't believe what I was hearing. Here my leg still hurt and I was working so hard and she was telling me that I was being a little baby. Michael Bivens of New Edition had seen me get hurt on television and had written me a letter, sent me a ton of CDs. Coach Summitt started harping on that.

"Look at this!" she said, waving around a CD. "Other people believe in you. People are counting on you! Chamique is being selfish! What are you going to do—the first time you get hurt, you're going to let people down? If you don't play in this game . . ." It went on and on.

I was in tears at that point. I was sitting in that chair, across from her big desk, and I was crying. With Coach Summitt, it was always a challenge. Always. And I never wanted her to be right when she said things like that to me. I didn't want her to be able to say that I was a baby, that I had let people down. I knew I was going to do it. Right there, I could see how much I'd grown up that year.

This was going to be *for me,* to prove something to myself. Not just to Coach Summitt. I could hardly run. But I wasn't going to quit.

I was maybe 80 percent in that first game, but as Coach Summitt told the media when they questioned her decision to play me, "Chamique at eighty percent is better than most people at a hundred." I heard that, and I thought, *She really believes in me.*

We played that first-round game at home, in Thompson-Boling Arena, and when I went out on the court for warm-ups, I immediately felt stiff-legged. So I went over to the bench where Coach Summitt was standing.

"Coach Summitt," I said. "I'm feeling a little stiff. Maybe I should come off the ball."

She just gave me this *look.*

"Holdsclaw," she said, "if you're gonna play, you'd better be ready to go."

I knew then that she wasn't going to accept any excuses.

I wore a brace, but my knee still hurt. Oh, it hurt. We were playing Radford, and we killed them by 41 points, so there wasn't too much pressure on me, but I managed to score 14 points and get 8 rebounds. Two nights later, against Ohio State, I scored 20.

By the time we went to the East Regionals in Charlottesville, I tried to give it everything I had, but I still didn't have that much mobility. Against Kansas in the semifinals, I was lucky. I was able to shoot over most of their players and I managed to pour in enough outside jumpers—and I went to the basket a few times too—to finish with 16 points in our 21-point win.

Virginia was smarter. Their coaching staff knew I wasn't mobile and wasn't attacking with my usual confidence. They could see it. So they put Demya Walker on to defend me. Demya was a freshman too, but she was six feet three inches tall and extremely tough. We were expected to beat Virginia pretty easily, but I wasn't moving well that night, and Demya definitely did her job.

We were playing in Charlottesville, so the crowd was against us, and we fell behind by 17 points. I wasn't scoring, and my teammates were trying to pick up the slack. We shot so poorly in the first half that we only scored 14 points—14 points!—and I thought Coach Summitt was going to explode at halftime. She didn't even ask us to go back out there and win. She just told us to show some pride and try not to be an embarrassment.

Despite the trouble I'd had all game, I still wanted the ball when we got into the stretch. I managed to put in a jumper during a 12–0 run, and we took control of the game. We ended up with a 52–46 victory, and all of a sudden, we were on our way to Charlotte—my first Final Four!—after all.

My knee still hurt when we got to Charlotte, but I was so excited. This was the hometown of Tiffani Johnson, and there were tons of people around, people to cheer for us. I knew my knee was still bad, but I also knew I had to produce. Coach Summitt worried that I was distracted. I'd been named a Kodak All-American and freshman of the year around that time, which is why I had to go to the Final Four banquet and these extra press conferences, and everything was a little crazy. So pretty soon Coach Summitt called me in for a meeting.

Uh-oh was my immediate thought. *What did I do now?*

"Chamique," she said, "you are too distracted. You are supposed to be focusing on the game. Maybe it's easy for a freshman to be happy just to be here, but at Tennessee we don't tolerate that. We're here to win."

I tried to tell her that I couldn't help it, that I was expected to attend these things. But the look she gave me stopped me cold. Once again, I knew what she was thinking: *No excuses. None.* So I did my duty and went to things I had to go to, but I made sure Coach Summitt always knew I was focused, especially in practice. She was right—I didn't want just to be there either, I wanted to win a championship.

In the semifinals, we played Connecticut, which was a huge deal. The rivalry we had with UConn was huge, and we had been on the losing end of it lately. They'd beaten us three straight times, including in the national championship game the year before, when they went undefeated. Things had been said between players and coaches, and so a lot of people on the team really wanted this badly. They'd also beaten us in January, on our own court. Needless to say, we wanted blood.

The game was bitter. We kept taking the lead and they kept fighting back—twice they recovered from double-digit deficits—and they had to get a 3-pointer at the buzzer from Nykesha Sales just to send it into overtime. The star of the game, though, was Michelle, who stepped up huge. She just took over the game, driving in the lane, outplaying Jennifer Rizzotti when it really counted. Nykesha had 28 points—her best ever—and we still won by 5. It almost felt like a miracle, because Connecticut had this twenty-game winning streak and everyone was expecting them to take us again.

For the rest of my career at Tennessee, I used that game against UConn to draw on whenever we played them again. Maybe it's because I wasn't there for that loss in the 1995 championship game, but I always told our players to let it go; we had beaten them in crunch time the following year, and that was all that mattered. So what if they beat us in the regular season? It's who wins in the postseason that matters, and this time, we'd beaten them.

Georgia beat Stanford in the other semifinal, so we were going to have to face another team we'd lost to that season—Georgia beat us in Athens in January—in the championship. Georgia had been so happy to see us knock off UConn that their players were giving us high fives as we left the court and they went on to play Stanford. We were happy, but when we saw Georgia win, we knew we had a tough final ahead of us. Georgia had the best player in the country, Saudia Roundtree, a senior who had been named the Naismith Player of the Year for women, almost unanimously.

Roundtree was an incredible player, and it was going to be up to Latina Davis to guard her. I didn't envy Latina that task, but she did an amazing job. Saudia went 3-of-14 from the floor and only had 8 points. We won pretty easily, 83–65. I led our team in scoring with 16 points, and had 14 rebounds too, but I really felt like it was Latina who won the game for us. Afterward, Coach Summitt said that as a team we played nearly a perfect game, and that was something, coming from her.

It's hard to describe what it felt like to stand out there on the court after the final buzzer, with all those people cheering, and we're all hugging one another and jumping up and down and screaming. Every year in high school I'd won the championship, but it was nothing like this.

We had a party that night. What a party. We were up all night long, laughing, talking, cracking jokes. I was so excited. My grandmother was there. Davon was there, having a ball. I couldn't even feel the pain in my knee anymore. And that's when I realized Coach Summitt had just taught me a lesson. There were two things she always said. One was "Tough times don't last, but tough people do." The other one was "If you put in the hard work, if you pay the price, it will pay off." After winning that championship, I felt like I could accomplish anything. It was the greatest feeling in the world.

MICKIE DEMOSS ON CHAMIQUE

At times, I think, Chamique would get overwhelmed by things. She would let things pile up, so she got behind in her schoolwork, and then maybe she overcommitted herself socially, and then maybe she was struggling on the basketball court at the same time, and it would all be too much. Pat would get on her, and she'd just lose it. She'd get so frustrated.

It never really was one particular thing. It was usually when the whole world piled up on her. Then Pat would start yelling at her at practice, and she wouldn't know how to deal with it. She'd say, "I'm going to quit, I'm going to go home. I can never please her." And I always wondered: *Why this time? Why today when Pat yelled at her and not yesterday? Why is this the moment that sent her over the edge?*

It took a while to understand that Chamique internalizes everything. She lets things build and build and build and doesn't turn to anyone to help her out. That's why, when the next little thing hits—and it could be something as minor as being asked why she didn't turn in her practice gear—Chamique would be overwhelmed. You have to understand, Chamique had a few more things to juggle than your normal college student.

She liked to stay in her comfort zone, and that meant she was a loner sometimes. That was hard for us to balance on the team. You want to respect that in her to a certain degree, but all the other players looked to her so much. They needed some type of interaction. They always wanted to rally behind Chamique.

I look at her now and I am so proud. The little things she does are unbelievable. She bought Christmas presents for the staff here. She came to the Final Four and had presents for the whole team. She sat in the stands and cheered for us and wore Michelle Snow's jersey as a sign of support. We've never had a former player that has given back to the program the way she has. A player of her stature still feeling the need to come back and be a part of her college program and help out her college players—well, that just warms my heart.

Chapter 7

*Chamique and Kellie Jolly with Lady Vols
friend Gerry Campbell.*

Sophomore year was my hardest on the basketball court. We graduated two seniors the spring before—Michelle Marciniak and Latina Davis—and most of our starters, besides me, were juniors. I think we felt the loss of that senior leadership right away, and people were looking to me to fill the void. Coach Summitt didn't say that at first. She'd say we had upperclassmen to lead us, but I found out soon enough that she thought otherwise. Getting this team back to a national championship was going to be my job.

It was a big one. The first terrible thing to happen to our team that year happened before the season even started. It was only October when Kellie Jolly tore the anterior cruciate ligament in her right knee. Kellie was supposed to take over for Michelle Marciniak in the backcourt, and now here we were, starting the season without her as well. She wouldn't be ready to play until early January. That seemed like a long, long way away.

Coach Summitt started riding me again, all the time, from our very first practices. We had built a pretty good relationship, I thought, and she had been dealing with me one-on-one most of the time, but I think maybe she had realized how much I was going to have to do to take this team to another championship. So right from the beginning, she started demanding more of me. And not knowing where that was coming from, I got frustrated really fast.

We were still in October—the season doesn't start until November—when we had our first really big blowup. We were working out in the physical education building and Coach Summitt got on me really hard about my academics, putting pressure on me to do more, get better grades, all of that. She was really forceful, all over me.

"Chamique!" she yelled. "You're not taking school seriously enough. You're here to get a degree and I'm not putting up with any of this from you. You're going to work harder."

She went on and on and on, and I was really upset because I thought I'd been doing well in school. She always challenged me. She didn't accept an average performance at anything, and she wasn't going to let me just go about things without focus. If she found out I wasn't communicating with my teachers, she got on me. If she found out I wasn't sitting in the front of the class— Coach Summitt had this rule that we all had to sit in the first three rows—she was on me. I know it was for my own good. That time, though, she just pushed me too far.

Mickie interfered then, took me into this little office off the court and tried to calm me down. I was crying, and I told her I wasn't going to practice, I wasn't ever going to practice again, I was just going home.

"I can't take this anymore, I just can't take it," I told Mickie. "You can't talk me out of this. I'm going home. I'm calling my grandmother. I'm getting ready to go home right now."

Mickie didn't try to change my mind. She kept saying things like "Okay, okay, why don't you go back to your room and call your grandmother. And you let me know how you want to pack your stuff up and get it home. And is your grandmother going to come and get you, or do we need to make arrangements?" She kept going on and on, being supportive, not disagreeing with me at all. I guess she was trying to use reverse psychology, but I was so upset that day I wasn't even paying much attention.

We were in that little office until practice was at least half over, and I knew my teammates were aware that I was in there all upset and crying, so there was no way I was going to go out there and finish practice. No way. I didn't want to be embarrassed, look bad. So I left. I went back to my room, and all I could think was *I'm out of here.* I was furious. And when Mickie called me later, I was still upset and frustrated, and I didn't want to talk about it, not yet.

The truth was, though, I didn't think I could leave. Something within myself always kept me there. I've never been a quitter. I just couldn't handle the way Coach Summitt got on me sometimes.

Mickie told me I needed to talk to Coach Summitt alone and try to straighten things out. Once I had calmed down and started to think about things logically again, I knew she was right. So I talked to Coach Summitt and we worked it out and we moved on. Once again, I realized that what I needed from Coach Summitt— what I always need—was to know what's expected of me. Instead of yelling at me for not doing something in school, or something on the court, just out of the blue, I need her to sit down and tell me what she expects from me. And then I'll do everything I can to accomplish that. I'm the kind of person who needs direction and discipline, and Coach Summitt was great about discipline, but sometimes I needed her to be more specific about her directions.

I wish I could say that was the low point of the year, but it wasn't. This was going to be one tough season. The games started, and right away there were nights when it was crunch time and the ball would just come to me, and only me, again and again and again. No one else wanted to take responsibility. I always felt like I was shooting for us to win, the team on my back. I couldn't pass up shots, because we didn't have the talent we'd had the year before. We had to play great defense to be competitive because we weren't as offensively gifted. It felt like I had so much on my shoulders, so much of the time.

We didn't play well a lot of the time. We lost ten games that season—the most any Tennessee team had lost in more than a decade. I wasn't used to losing. I'd only lost four games my entire four years at Christ the King, and even the four losses we'd had my freshman season at Tennessee seemed like too many. Every single one of them had hurt me. The ten we lost sophomore year hurt even more.

We lost for the first time just four games into the season, to Louisiana Tech in the Women's Pre-Season National Invitational Tournament. We got down by 18 points in the first half, and nothing I did could save us. I scored 26 points that night, grabbed 13 rebounds, but I was the only player in double digits. We lost by 2. It worried me a lot.

Things got worse in early December, when we lost to Georgia and Stanford at home in back-to-back games. I'm not sure I could remember ever having lost two games in a row before in my life, and I felt like the team was in trouble. I kept thinking, *Consistency, consistency. We need to find some consistency.* But it's a lot easier to realize that than it is to make it happen.

The Georgia game was a big test for us. It was a rematch of our national title game from the year before, only they didn't have Roundtree anymore—and we didn't have nearly the same team we'd had, either. I scored a career-high 34 points that night, and 15 of those points came in the last three minutes of regulation, when I went nuts trying to pull us out of a double-digit deficit. Thompson-Boling Arena was crazy. It was exciting, and everything seemed to go by so quickly. I remember I found Tiffani Johnson under the basket and she put it in and we went into overtime. I scored 8 more points then, but we still lost by 1.

I was less frustrated after that game than I was after most of our losses. We fought hard that game. I was disappointed, but for a change I really felt like we had given it everything we had. Still, those two losses came right before finals, so at the time it seemed like we went forever without a victory. Actually, it was only two weeks. But it was a long two weeks. And I admit it wasn't easy to focus on school with all the pressure I was feeling with the team.

We lost back-to-back games again in early January, right before Kellie came back. First we had to go to Connecticut to play UConn in a game that was on national television, and we got killed by 15 points. We went straight from there to Old Dominion, which was ranked number two in the country at the time. We lost to them by double digits too. I scored 27 points that night, and once again, it didn't make a difference. I was devastated that night. I sobbed in the locker room; I just couldn't stop myself. Coach Summitt said we'd played hard, but it was of little comfort to me then.

It got to the point where my teammates would apologize to me in the locker room after we lost games. They'd say, "Chamique, we're sorry, we know we didn't give you enough support." They even wrote me notes. It drove me crazy. I didn't want apologies. I didn't want excuses. I just wanted them to play harder. My response was always the same. "Don't tell me this! Just come to play!"

Off the court, things were better for me sophomore year. I got my first car. Actually, I got my license, and then I got the car. Kim and I went car shopping together, picked out identical Dodge Neons, only in different colors. Mine was black, hers was red. I got the money from my family—from my grandmother and my dad. My uncle Thurman had promised to buy me a car sophomore year, and it made me sad to think about that. I still missed him.

Coach Summitt used to give me so much grief about my driving. I admit, I didn't have a lot of experience. I never drove in New York, that's for sure. But the day I got my new car, I drove it out to Coach Summitt's house for a team dinner. She lived on a cul-de-sac and I was practicing my driving, down the block and back, and she watched me. Then she came out to the car and looked at me, shaking her head.

"Chamique!" she said. "Why in the world did you get a stick?"

"But Coach Summit," I answered, "it's an automatic!"

She just started laughing, teasing me about how my driving was so jerky. She said I kept speeding up, slowing down, speeding up, slowing down, so she thought it had to be a stick shift. There was no other explanation. She told me she was never—*never*—going to ride in the car with me.

Kim and Zakiyah and all my teammates teased me about my driving too. They said it took me thirty minutes to parallel-park. I didn't care. I was still learning. Getting that car changed my life dramatically. I'd always felt a little trapped in Knoxville, with nothing to do to fill my free time. Now I could go places without having to bum rides off my friends. I went to the mall a lot. I'd just drive around too. Anything to get out. It made me feel freer than I had my whole first year at Tennessee.

Sophomore year—the end of sophomore year, actually—is also when I got my first real boyfriend.

I admit I started to get a lot more interested in guys in college. It helped that my girlfriends at school were not all from the basketball team, so they were out there more, socializing. They could tell me what was going on. They used to tease me too, for not having dated much in high school.

My freshman year I liked this one guy so much. I had a huge crush on him. We dated for about two months, I guess, and then he told me that he wanted to date other girls too. I was pretty upset about that. It didn't seem like the kind of situation I wanted to be in. But I admit, I was insecure and the first thing I started thinking was *What's the matter with me? What did I do wrong?* Girls always seem to do that—try to figure out what they did wrong, when a lot of times we just have to realize that he just wasn't the greatest guy. He came back around eventually—the next year— and was pressing me to go out, but I didn't want him anymore. He told me he loved me, I remember that. And I said, "How could you love me? We haven't even been together that much." My teammates teased me about him, kept saying that I loved him too, but we never really were more than good friends.

I was the type of girl in college that all the guys were cool with. There are girls that guys try to dog over and there are girls that guys want to get with because they respect them, and I always worked hard to be that type of girl. I was a "good girl." I believe in getting to know a person. I want to talk to guys, hang out with them, become friends first. That's what happened with Larry.

Larry Williams was my first real boyfriend. I met him on my college recruiting visit, actually. I went to the Foot Locker at the mall, and he worked there, and he was friendly and invited me and some of the other girls to a party. He went to Knoxville College, played football. I didn't go to the party, and I really didn't think much about him after that.

We ran into each other again when I started school the next fall. I was in Foot Locker again—I do a lot of shopping!—and there he was. And that's when we became friends.

We were friends for almost two years before we started dating. That's part of why I felt so comfortable around him. I got to know him as a person first, and even though I was pretty much "Chamique" and everything from the day I got on campus, when I met him it hadn't become a really big thing yet. I could still go to the grocery store and not be bothered, stuff like that. So I felt like Larry knew me for who I was, and not just as a basketball player. Besides, he was cute and sweet and treated me well.

It was a big deal when I invited him to Astoria that summer. My grandmother knew I always talked about him in our phone calls, and she had figured out that we spent a lot of time together. But I'd never brought a boyfriend home before, so I was nervous.

My family liked him. Everyone seemed to get along from the beginning, and I liked that. He was good to Davon. He would call my grandmother "ma'am" all the time, which I think made her a little suspicious, but I think she gave him credit for trying to be respectful and polite.

This was my first real relationship. And the first one, because you're young, you pretty much think you're going to be with that person forever. I know that's how I felt about Larry. We were together for two and a half years, and when you spend that kind of time with a person, they know almost everything about you. They share almost every moment. And with Tennessee being as small and slow as it was to me, we spent even more time together. He would go to work—he is two years older and had graduated, but he stayed in Knoxville afterward—and I would go to school and practice, and then we'd just hang out and be together in the evenings. We'd watch movies or watch TV. Anything.

He was there to celebrate with me when we won our big games and he was there when I lost in the NCAA Tournament my senior year. We shared everything. He was a big part of my support system, right from the beginning.

* * *

By the middle of the season, Coach Summitt and I had another sit-down meeting, but this one wasn't because we weren't getting along. She wanted to talk to me about the struggles we were having as a team, and what she needed me to do.

I told her that I had been trying to be a leader out there, only it never seemed to work. I was frustrated because I needed my teammates and I didn't feel like they were always there. Coach Summitt told me it was my job to lead them. "You guys talk all the time off the court," she said. "How come you can't communicate once you're on it?" I told her I'd do everything I could.

"Don't quit," she told me. "Don't quit on this team, and one day you'll realize how much you're able to accomplish."

Things didn't really turn around, though. Some of our practices were really ugly. I was frustrated, and as always, I was taking out my frustrations on the court. I'd lose my temper sometimes, have outbursts, yell at people. Coach Summitt would have practice players beating on me, pounding me, making me feel the way it was going to be in the game—I was always getting double-teamed then—and sometimes it got to be too much. I'd throw the ball, kick it, and Coach Summitt would start yelling again.

"This is why we stink!" she'd say. "Because we don't work hard in practice! We don't work hard."

My teammates and I, we'd look at one another sometimes and just say, "Wow, she's crazy!" But that was just Coach Summitt. She was as frustrated as the rest of us.

We lost back-to-back games to end the regular season—to Louisiana State and Louisiana Tech—both on the road, and didn't even have a strong enough record to get a bye in the first round of the SEC Tournament. That was a little humiliating. But the humiliation was about to get worse. We won our first two games in the tournament to make it to the SEC championship game, where we were going to face Auburn. We'd beaten Auburn barely more than a week before, without a whole lot of trouble, so I was feeling pretty confident. Besides, Auburn wasn't even ranked anymore, they'd had such a rough season.

The game was played in Chattanooga, and I don't know what

happened to us. We were tied at halftime, stayed close the whole game, but we couldn't finish. We lost control of the ball in the final minutes, and ended up with a 61–59 defeat. It was our tenth defeat, and it knocked us out of the Top Ten rankings by the Associated Press. I didn't know what that was going to mean when the NCAA Tournament selection committee handed out the postseason seedings, but I knew it wasn't good.

What I wasn't prepared for was the onslaught I got from Coach Summitt when we returned home from Chattanooga. She called me into her office and took me apart, blaming me—and me only—for the loss.

"We lost because you didn't take over, Chamique!" she yelled at me. "You didn't step up. You didn't do your job. The girl scored the winning basket on *you*. That's your burden!"

I was stunned. All I kept thinking during her tirade was *She thinks it's my fault. She thinks it's my fault.* I felt terrible. I was crying again. It seems like I spent a lot of days crying in Coach Summitt's office. But I was mad too. Furious. I felt like it was me against the world.

When I look back now, I realize that this was just another example of Coach Summitt knowing what buttons to push with me. She knew I had a lot of pride, and if she made me believe I'd been responsible for our loss, I'd be driven—really *driven*—in the tournament. My grandmother always tells me that I take my anger and my frustrations out on the basketball court, and Coach Summitt was giving me some anger and frustration to burn. I walked out of her office feeling like I had icicles in my veins. I was ready to go, to really prove something. I was so focused, I was seeing red. And that's exactly how Coach Summitt wanted me to feel.

It's amazing to me what happened after that. After being a team that seemed to have so little chemistry all season, we bonded. We really came together. It was the most exciting experience I've ever had in terms of finding true character in my teammates. We reached down inside, those few weeks in March, and we found out what we were made of. And we were made of strong stuff.

We still got home court for the first two rounds of the NCAA Tournament, and we beat Grambling State in the first game, but lost Kellie for the second half to an ankle injury. Two nights later, we beat Oregon, with Kellie managing to play a few minutes. We were headed to the regionals. I was starting to feel so much better about our team, but I knew we still were considered huge underdogs when it came to repeating as national champions.

We were sent to Iowa City, where we had Connecticut looming. First, though, we had to beat Colorado, which we did. Then we faced the Huskies, who were undefeated, 33–0. The coaching staff stayed up all night preparing for that game, but I just kept telling my teammates: "We beat them last year in the postseason, we can do it again." And we did, by 10 points. I was named the Midwest Regional most valuable player, but that mattered nothing compared to how we were playing. We were playing without fear for the first time.

The Final Four was in Cincinnati that year, and we had to face Notre Dame in the semifinals. We'd beaten Notre Dame already that season, and we were playing so well that I was pretty confident. I played one of my best games of the season. I had 31 points and felt like I was scoring from all over the place. No one could stop me. No one could stop us. One more win and we'd be on top of the mountain again.

Despite being the defending champions, we were underdogs to Old Dominion, and I think a lot of us were nervous. That whole season, HBO had been following us around, making a documentary. At times it made me feel uncomfortable, especially when they were in the locker room during our rough periods. By the Final Four, though, I liked it. I felt like we could become this amazing story—a team that lost ten games but still came together to win it all.

On the bus ride to the championship game in Cincinnati, Coach Summitt played a clip from the film in progress on the VCR, and it was of the night we had lost to Old Dominion. You could see us all there in the locker room afterward, devastated. The film was set to the song "Only the Strong Survive." I just kept thinking that I didn't want to feel that way again. It gave me fire. You watch how we were after that game—crying, crushed—and you want to do anything you can to keep from having to experience that another time. It was motivation for me.

I had my nails painted neon orange and I wore my orange mouth guard—I had braces by then—and I was so pumped for this game. I wanted a second championship more than anyone could imagine. When we took the court, I was aggressive immediately, scoring three quick baskets to get us out to an 8–4 lead. We were up by 15 at one point in the first half. Things looked good, and at halftime, I told Coach Summitt: "I'll be ready." No matter what happened, I was determined to carry our team that night.

Old Dominion came back, and came back hard. They took the lead from us three times in the second half, the last time with about seven minutes left in the game. I knew this was when Coach Summitt expected me to take charge. She always says that the more pressure there is in a game, the better I play. That's how I felt that night.

So I took charge, with more than a little help from Kellie. Every time I got open, Kellie seemed to get the ball to me. She gave me a lead for a layup, she hit me from out of bounds, she lobbed over the defense to find me inside. We took charge, and when the final buzzer sounded, we'd won, 68–59.

I was the one to climb the ladder and finish cutting down the net, and I hung it around my neck and wore it like a necklace. After all we'd been through that season, it was an incredible moment. Coach Summitt called it the most improbable of the five national championships she'd won as head coach at Tennessee, and I'd have to agree with her. She also called me the best player in the country. I said, "No, no, it's Nykesha Sales."

"No, Chamique," she said, looking me right in the eye. "It's *you*."

Coach Summitt and I have talked a lot about what happened that season. She admitted that there were times during that year when she felt helpless, and she was sure I must have felt helpless too. She said she was so proud of me, though, because I'd listened to what she'd told me in her office that day and I hadn't quit on this team. I never gave up.

I grew up a lot that season. I began to realize that instead of getting frustrated when things are hard, you have to recognize that everything that happens in your life is meant to teach you something. That season taught me to be committed to something, no matter what. It taught me patience. I liked that. Sometimes you may have what you think is too hard a struggle, but if you just dig in and commit yourself, you never know what might happen.

That night was also the first time that I'd been drunk in my life. We had Dom Pérignon, and I drank almost an entire bottle by myself, and ended up throwing up out my nose. It was horrible. The next morning, my head was killing me. I kept telling everyone, "I'll never drink like that again." I'll have a glass of wine or something when I go out to dinner. Or I'll have a glass of champagne. But I don't really drink. I don't like beer, and I've never had hard liquor.

I guess I was like other kids when I was growing up. I'd have a glass of wine at my grandmother's on a special occasion like New Year's Eve, and I'd giggle about getting wine in church for the first time, when I was ten years old or something. I'd sneak a taste of somebody's beer at holiday parties when my relatives were all together. But I always thought it was nasty. And I never did get into the drinking parties that people would have in high school. I'd never go out with my friends and drink beer somewhere, or try a shot of vodka. I just wasn't interested.

I guess it's obvious that part of my decision not to drink comes from what I saw when I was little. My mom drank, my dad drank, and when they did, they'd argue, just like some of my neighbors did, and so many other people who were around. My grandmother's always telling me that my grandfather had a drinking problem, before I was even born. He had one, and then my parents, and I know it's in my system, it's in my family, and I'm not going to take any risks.

I've seen how people act when they're drunk, how they act differently. I'd watch people on campus get drunk and it would turn a great night into an uproar. People want to fight. People want to do stupid things. I don't have time for that. I can only be around people who understand that one is enough, or two. That you don't have to keep drinking, drinking, drinking until you don't even know who you are anymore.

I don't smoke, either, have never touched a cigarette. I'd probably die if I smoked, given how much I'm running around. My lungs would give out. When you're an athlete, why would you want to mess around with things like that?

Because I didn't do these things, my roommate used to tease me that I was square. And I used to make fun of myself, say I was a boring person. But I'm not boring. Maybe I'm square, but I'm not boring. I know how to have fun, how to have a good time. I like to hang out with my friends. I like to go to restaurants, anything with music. Not drinking doesn't make you boring. Anyone who thinks that is a joke.

This is what I chose for myself, in part because I've always been aware of my situation, and how I represent more than just myself—I represented my team at Tennessee, I represent my family always—and the image I should have. It's not that I'm going to stop living my life the way I want to, but I'm also not going to do anything dumb. I'm not going to succumb to anyone's peer pressure. I'm going to be a leader. I'm going to be the one to say "I don't need to do that."

Why would I want to go out and get drunk with people and then have to listen to someone say, "Oh, Chamique, when you were drunk, do you know you did this and you did that?" I don't need all that. I just like to have fun. And I have fun without it. I have fun shopping with my friends, hanging out, just joking. I have fun playing basketball. I don't need to drink to have fun.

I won a whole bunch of individual awards that spring and was named a finalist for several others, but I didn't pay too much attention to that. There was a lot going on in my life. I started dating Larry. I started talking to my mom a little bit more. I concentrated really hard on school. And I was invited to play on the women's U.S. national team for the summer tour.

Getting named to the team was a real honor. I was the youngest player by far. And I felt so out of place, and so awkward. I felt like I just didn't fit in that situation. Like I didn't belong.

I roomed with Teresa Edwards—the youngest player on the team rooming with the oldest. I suppose they did that so I had someone to look out for me. And I ended up really liking Teresa a lot. I really look up to her. But that was my main problem that summer—I looked up to all the players I was playing with, and never really felt like I was one of them. When you're playing basketball, you need to bond with your teammates. You need to really feel like you're a team.

We traveled to all kinds of places where I'd never been. Slovakia, Brazil, Germany. I was used to traveling so much with Tennessee, but not out of the country. This was new for me, and kind of fun. Learning to go through passport control, things like that. I used to ask the veteran players—ones who had played in the European leagues—to look at their passports. They had all these stamps from all over the world.

I was a little homesick too. Coach Summitt's assistant, Katie Wynn, sent me packages with sardines, hot sauce, crackers, bubble gum, all kinds of silly things inside. I called Mickie collect at Tennessee all the time. I don't even want to think about the phone bills! But I needed someone to talk to, and I didn't really feel like there was anyone on the team who filled that role.

I tried not to be too different, but I was. The other players had a different perspective on life, on everything. They'd done more than I had, seen more. Everything about what we liked was different. I'd play video games, and they'd read. I'd listen to hip-hop music on the bus, and they'd laugh at me. No one wanted to listen to what I listened to. I ended up sitting on the bus with my headphones on all the time, while everyone else around me was talking.

I'm sure that's why they put me in with Teresa, to try and smooth the transition. Maybe if I could get to know her, I would feel comfortable around everyone else, since she was the oldest and something of the team leader. I was hoping she'd make me feel better, make me feel like, "Okay, you're young, but you're pretty cool," but I don't think that ever really happened. I was still so young and so immature, and the things I'd say would be totally off the wall sometimes.

I don't think I really understood at the time how important the national team was to these players, especially the ones who had played in Atlanta at the Olympics the year before and had finally gotten a real national spotlight. The two new pro leagues had just formed—the ABL had played its first season, and the WNBA was playing that summer—and this was a direct result of the kind of contributions players like Teresa had made to the women's game. Soon, very soon, pro basketball would be a very big factor in my future. But that summer I was still just a college kid, dreaming of a third national championship.

KELLIE JOLLY HARPER ON CHAMIQUE

Chamique and I are very different. We come from two totally different backgrounds. One small-town Tennessee girl and one big-city girl from New York. Our relationship is unique. We could always talk about anything, but we knew each other so well that we didn't have to talk about anything at all. She never had to come in and explain what was going on with her, because I could almost read her mind. I knew when she had a bad day and when she had a good one. We just knew how to get along together, no matter how different we were. Our common bond was basketball.

As the point guard, it was my job to know the team inside and out, and that started with knowing Chamique. I needed to know who Chamique is, what makes her click, so that I could get the best out of her. On the court, Chamique is very smooth. That's the first word I'd use to describe her. She's very poised, and she's almost sneaky because she's so deceptive. It looks like she's not playing hard or scoring a lot of points and then you look up and she's got 20-something on the board.

Chamique always wanted the ball. That's the type of player she is. And I always knew when she wanted it, and where she wanted it; and in turn, she knew that I was going to get it to her. We had an incredible feel for each other. I could look at her sometimes and just *know* what she was going to do next. That's how well we knew each other.

The time we spent together was almost always around the team. We were so close, though, it was like we were sisters. We experienced so much together. It's hard to explain what it's like to be a basketball player at Tennessee. Harder still to explain what it was like to be Chamique in that world. Everywhere she went, people had a story to tell her about a game they saw, or a time they passed her in the grocery store, or the flight they took that she was on too. It's like they all just wanted a little piece of her. People just love Chamique. They love her so much, they want a piece of her to take away for themselves.

Chapter 8

Chamique and the Lady Vols speaking to the press after winning their third consecutive NCAA championship in 1998.

I didn't grow up with dreams of playing professional basketball for a very simple reason: women's professional basketball didn't exist in the United States when I was a kid. I watched the NBA, and I used to like to watch Scottie Pippen, Michael Jordan, Magic Johnson. I wanted to be like Magic Johnson. There weren't too many female athletes for me to look up to, certainly not on television. Jackie Joyner-Kersee was probably the one I followed most, and I wasn't even all that into track. I tried it for a while at Christ the King, but let's just say I'm not a big fan of five-mile runs.

By the time I was in high school, I kept an eye on women's college basketball and tried to see Rebecca Lobo whenever Connecticut was on television. Still, I didn't see basketball as my future. I saw basketball as my ticket to a college education. I was going to use the game to get myself a degree. Even when I was really young, growing up in a place where a lot of people didn't go to college, I always assumed I would go. That comes from my grandmother. I probably never realized it then, but as I look back on it now, I just as easily could have this mark on my chest that said, "I'm from a housing project." I could have used that as an

105

excuse. An excuse to have low expectations or to make tons of excuses, but I never did.

Basketball didn't save Chamique Holdsclaw. I don't want anyone to ever say that. Basketball just made it so that when I got to college—and I *knew* I was going to college—I made it on a scholarship. I thought about being a lawyer. I studied political science and public administration at Tennessee. And though she may not have always thought so, I listened when Coach Summitt reminded me that I was at Tennessee first and foremost to get my degree. School has always been important to me.

The whole landscape changed, though, when the two women's professional leagues formed in 1997, during my sophomore year. All of a sudden, basketball wasn't just a game for women, it could actually be a *career*. I'll never forget Coach Summitt looking at me one day that season and saying, almost offhand, "You know, Chamique, you can make a million dollars playing this game someday." I was floored. It was never something I had considered.

But by the start of my junior season, it wasn't something I could ignore. When we were in Cincinnati for the Final Four the previous spring, the talk already had started. Reporters would interview Kate Starbird from Stanford or Kara Wolters from Connecticut and want to know if they were going to pick the WNBA—which played in the summers only—or the ABL, which had a full season. Then they'd come to me and ask if I had considered leaving school after my junior season to jump to the pros. At first I was floored by the question, then I started to hear it so often I didn't know what to think. Sure, it was technically against the rules— both leagues said they wouldn't take underclassmen—but everyone was saying the leagues would break their rules for me. And if I wanted to take them to court? Forget it. The precedent had been set in the NBA.

On top of that, agents had started trying to get close to me sophomore year. They would try to approach me—it was against NCAA rules for us to have any contact—and they tried calling my grandmother too. People would tell me that they were talking about a lot of money. I tried to shrug it off, but that wasn't easy.

Coach Summitt could tell I was distracted, and she didn't want my status at Tennessee to be uncertain, so we had another one of our famous meetings at the start of junior year. She wanted to know what I was thinking. I confess now that I didn't understand how big the question was, and how much Coach Summitt thought it would be a distraction to the team if I wasn't firm in my decision. I told her what I honestly believed.

"I'm coming back for my senior year," I said. "I promised my grandmother I'd get my degree."

With the advice of Coach Summitt and some lawyers, my grandmother took out an insurance policy on me, with Lloyd's of London. I figured the issue was settled. But I guess I didn't give off that impression, because Coach Summitt told me later that she never felt fully confident in my commitment to stay at Tennessee that entire year.

The troops arrived junior year, and I was so excited. After begging Coach Summitt for help my whole sophomore season, I came back to this amazing recruiting class. We had four new freshmen coming in: Tamika Catchings, Semeka Randall, Ace Clement, and Teresa Geter. All of a sudden, instead of being "Mique," I was one of the "Three Meeks"—me, Tamika, and Semeka. I loved it.

After sophomore year, I knew in my mind what I was capable of doing, but when I looked around at the new players that fall, I realized how happy I was to have help. I needed to have teammates I could pass to when I was getting double-teamed. I needed players around me who were going to help me work on my game, make it stronger. When we won the title the previous spring, everyone was saying that "Holdsclaw stepped it up a notch," and I was proud of that, but I was thrilled to see Semeka and Tamika and all the new faces that first day.

Coach Summitt wanted me to know that this was "my team," but after all the responsibility I'd shouldered the previous season, I'm not sure I really wanted that. She made an obvious concession to me when she assigned upperclassmen to watch out for each of our new rookies and didn't assign anyone to me. It was like she knew she needed to give me a little space.

Things were a little awkward with all of us in the beginning, and

I guess it was partly my fault, though I couldn't see it then. I had grown up so much my sophomore year, and even more with all the time I spent around the older players on the national team. Coach Summitt says I changed the most between sophomore and junior years. She's probably right.

I moved out of the dorms that fall and into an apartment with Zakiyah. I wanted more peace and more privacy. I started to treat basketball like business. I'd come to practice focused and prepared, put in a strong effort, and then just leave. I didn't hang out with the team the way I had. Though I loved playing with the Meeks on the court, I felt like I had grown up a lot after two years in college and experienced a lot of things they were just beginning to experience. So, mostly I was keeping to myself or spending time with my roommate, Zakiyah. That bothered people. The younger players felt I was being distant. My teammates began to think I was taking too much space for myself.

Things came to a head pretty quickly. I was arguing with Kyra Elzy—she was a sophomore guard on the team—and the younger players were feeling neglected by me. So Coach Summitt forced us all to have a meeting without any of the coaches involved. She had told me already that I needed to understand I was partly responsible to our recruiting class—that Semeka and Tamika had come to Tennessee because they wanted the opportunity to play with me, and I needed to understand and respect that. Still, I was feeling too much pressure to be everything for everybody. I wanted to be left alone.

We had it out in that meeting. It lasted for hours. Kyra and I settled our differences, and then I listened to Tamika try to explain how harsh she thought I was being and how distant. She said she wasn't even sure she wanted to be my friend.

I tried to explain that I was coming from a different perspective. That I had a lot of things I had to deal with now—the agents coming around, the talk about going pro, the fact that I couldn't walk down the street in Knoxville without getting stopped, let alone eat a meal in a restaurant in peace. But I wasn't getting my point across until Kellie stepped in.

Kellie is amazing. She understood me. She told me, "Mique, don't worry, you've grown up, you've matured. That's a *good* thing." Then she interfered on my behalf. In that way she has—and she is so much better at this than I am—Kellie made the younger players see my perspective. It also helped me a lot to know that she was behind me, that she knew I was really focused on basketball now, and that the team had to let me accomplish what I knew I could accomplish my way.

Kellie and I are so different. We come from entirely different worlds—she's from a small town in Tennessee, where there are about four thousand people and all of them love country music. I come from a housing project in New York City. How different could you be? We talk differently, we like different music, we like different things, but somehow we just bonded right from the first day we met, when we both were on our recruiting visits. Maybe it's because we sat there and talked about how many championships we were going to win together and she saw it the same way I did. Of course we were going to win—what else could possibly happen?

Kellie is a country diva, and I still tease her about that. She'll do her hair and I joke, "Oh, you think you're so fly!" I remember one time, we went to New York together to be on *The Rosie O'Donnell Show,* and Kellie just seemed so out of place in New York. "Kellie," I said, "now you're a big-city girl."

The *Rosie* show booked us two rooms in the hotel, but we stayed in one, and after the taping, I took her on an adventure. She rode a subway for the first time in her life. I took her to get New York pizza. I took her in her first New York cab. I took her to Macy's. She was awed by all of it.

Of course, Kellie has her stories about me too. I'd never ridden a horse before I went to visit Kellie in Sparta one summer. Her horse is named May Pine and I suppose I should have been scared or nervous or maybe a little bit cautious, but I wasn't. I just got on that horse and went riding. We went into a field—it was her uncle's land—and I asked her about the bales of hay everywhere. Only I didn't know they were bales. And I didn't know it was hay.

Kellie laughed harder than I'd ever seen her laugh. Apparently, everyone is supposed to know what bales of hay look like. I didn't. It's not something you see in Astoria.

Actually, Kellie and I didn't spend much time hanging out together outside of basketball. We almost never did anything that didn't have to do with a team function. But when you're committed to a program the way we all were committed at Tennessee, your team becomes your family—the players become your sisters—and that's what made Kellie and me so close. We had a lot of the same ideas, but our approach was always different. I'm the type who is going to do things my way—maybe it will be spontaneous, but it will get done. Kellie does things by the textbook. Together, though, we knew we could lead this team.

As the season went on, we learned to trust one another on the court, and I started to trust more off it. I was opening up to my teammates slowly, letting them get to know me. We'd joke and laugh and fool around on our road trips. Kellie and I took the role of team leaders and everybody just fell in.

At times I felt like we were America's team, riding this unbelievable streak, playing basketball like nobody had seen a women's college team play it before. We were so quick and so graceful and so fluid. Each one of us made the others look better. Each one of us knew her role, understood it, lived it. If someone was having a rough night—including me—the other players knew exactly how and when to pick up the slack. Teams could no longer just focus on me in the clutch moments, assuming that I would get the ball. We had so many weapons.

When I want to describe that team, I have to start with the General. That would be Kellie. She knew the game so well, and she could tear it apart. She was a coach on the floor for us. She knew everybody's strengths and everybody's weaknesses. Kellie is not going to give you the ball if you're not in a place where you're comfortable. She knew how to keep the game in control.

Semeka was our two guard. She brought great open floor ability to our team, and she was nasty on defense. She was so tenacious. Then there was me, at small forward, and then, at the fourth spot, you had Tamika Catchings. For a freshman, her game was unbelievable. She rebounded, she scored, she just played hard and did a little bit of everything. You always knew she was going to give it her all for forty minutes.

LaShonda Stephens played center for us, and she struggled with a knee problem for most of the season. But she was solid. She was a good defender and did a good job scoring from the high post.

Off the bench, we had another freshman, Teresa Geter—we called her Tree—who was a really diverse player, and then we had Kyra Elzy and Niya Butts. Ace Clement backed up Kellie. She was still learning to play the point. Even our walk-ons were a big part of our team, because they were there on the bench, cheering for us. They came to practice to play hard every day.

Off the court, Semeka—you could tell by the way she plays— was the outgoing one, who liked to pick the music we played on the bus. Ace was talkative too. And Niya, Kyra, and LaShonda all lived together, so they were pretty close. But we all got along that year and had a lot of fun together.

The most amazing thing, though, was the way we meshed on a basketball court. Together, it was like we could do anything. It was incredible to watch, and even more incredible to be a part of.

The best thing, I think, was how much we enjoyed playing together. I think that was obvious, right from our first pickup games before official practices started. The more we played together, though, the more obvious it became. People watching us could see it. There was this joy we took in being out there. We just had so much fun.

I admit that I became the nervous one as our undefeated ride went on and on. The freshmen didn't know any better—they didn't realize, I think, how incredible everything was. I worried that we were getting too arrogant, that we'd get so wrapped up into thinking we were unbeatable that we'd let down our guard and somebody would come in and smack us down. I used to harp on that all the time in the locker room.

"They're good! They're good!" I'd say about the next team we were going to play, no matter where they were ranked at the moment.

The younger players would scoff at me, talk trash.

"We're going to kick their butts!" they'd answer. "They can't handle us. Nobody can handle us!"

I'd grow more and more nervous when I heard things like that. *Uh-oh,* I'd think. *Are we taking this seriously enough? Are we setting ourselves up for a fall?*

I thought for certain that I was right and somebody was going to come along and knock us off our pedestal. Turns out I was wrong.

We were on a road trip to DePaul in January when I met Michael Jordan.

People started referring to me as "the female Michael Jordan" my sophomore season, I guess, and it didn't hurt that I wore his number, 23. I admit, I picked that number because of Jordan, but my grandmother quickly caught me and told me I should be more humble. Psalm 23, she said, should be my inspiration. I read it and knew she was right. That psalm is the one that begins "The Lord is my shepherd; there is nothing I shall want," and includes the passage "He guides me along the right path; he is true to his name. If I should walk in the valley of darkness, no evil would I fear."

Like anyone, I had admired Jordan's game for years, so when Coach Summitt announced that she had a surprise for us—a trip to Jordan's business office in Chicago—I was pretty thrilled. We'd been to Jordan's restaurant the night before, and I guess some of the players had been hounding Coach Summitt about meeting him. Apparently she had some clout, because we got in to see him the very next day.

Right away he singled me out, calling me by my nickname.

"What's up, Mique?" Michael said. Then he floored me with this: "I want to play you one-on-one."

I admit, I was flattered. I was in awe. Michael Jordan wanted to play against *me.* Michael Jordan was using my nickname. But I had to play it cool. And I was amused when he started giving me the Nike pitch.

"You're blinding me with all that Adidas!" he yelled at us, because at Tennessee we got our shoes from Adidas. "Mique, you've got to sign with Nike!"

Maybe he was giving me the soft sell, I don't know, but I thought it was funny. And I remember he warned me later, "It's all business after this. Enjoy it while you can." We hung out in his office for about half an hour, and a lot of my teammates got autographs and stuff like that.

That night, I called my grandmother.

"Grandma," I said, "guess who I met today?"

"Who?" she asked.

"Michael Jordan," I told her.

Grandma whooped.

"Did you get his autograph?" she asked me.

"Grandma," I replied, drawing her name out. "It's *only* Michael Jordan."

On my end of the phone, I smiled. I had to be cool.

By the end of the regular season, we had started to capture the attention of the whole country, and though it got to be a bit much at times, I recognized how great it was for women's basketball. Our HBO documentary came out near the end of the regular season, and then Coach Summitt's first book, an autobiography called *Reach for the Summit,* was published and made it to the bestseller list. Coach Summitt was on the cover of *Sports Illustrated*—the picture of her was scary, and we teased her about it relentlessly—and we were getting more and more airtime on ESPN and CNN/SI. By the time the tournament rolled around, the television morning shows were interested in us too. We even got our own line of sportswear, from Adidas.

Women's college basketball had been making really fast and really big strides in popularity, and I have to admit, even though we were their rivals, the undefeated season Connecticut had with Rebecca Lobo in 1995 had opened a lot of people's eyes to how advanced our game had become. Still, I'd always been something of a critic of women's basketball, having grown up playing with the guys on the courts in Astoria. I would readily admit that even with the advent of the ABL and the WNBA, I usually watched the NBA when I wanted to watch the game. I liked the athleticism of the men's game so much. And that's why I was really pleased when reporters started recognizing the athleticism of our Tennessee team that season, and people started writing that we could change the way people view the women's game. Having grown up dead tired of hearing people say things like, "She plays like a girl," it seemed like a great step to me.

As soon as I could get a copy, I read Coach Summitt's book, and it had a big impact on me. I went up to her on the team bus one day, sat down, and told her that I thought I finally understood her. She laughed and told me she would have written a book three years earlier if she'd known that was all it would take to get us on the same page.

By that point, though, Coach Summitt and I truly had an understanding. She knew how to motivate me, and I knew what she wanted me to do on the court. Sure, there were still times when she got on my case—like the point in the middle of the season when she tried to humiliate me for not playing enough defense—but for the most part, we had become very close.

Our relationship was so good, in fact, that my teammates had decided that I was the one who knew Coach Summitt's weak spots, and they used that fact. Whenever we wanted something—to eat at a particular restaurant, or to take a shopping trip while we were on the road—they'd always send me up to ask. I was their little emissary, sent to face the queen of intimidation. Only she didn't intimidate me all that much anymore.

For me, it's always been important for people to earn your trust. Coach Summitt had my respect from the first day I came to Knoxville, because she was my coach and she deserved that. But like anyone in my life, she had to earn my trust. And that took more time. But once we reached that point, and we did, our communication went to another level. I felt like she understood me, and understood what drives me inside. And that's not something that many people figure out.

We rolled through the regular season without a loss, won the SEC title, and were ready for the tournament to begin. Michael Jordan remembered us by sending a telegram to Knoxville before we started the tournament. "Good luck in the tournament and your undefeated season," it read. He signed it "Michael."

I decided once the postseason started that I wanted to make my own documentary to have as a keepsake. So I carried my handheld video camera with me everywhere—to practices, into the locker room, on the planes, when we went out to eat. Nobody was safe.

For the first few rounds, that tournament was a blast. We were strong, we felt invincible, we laughed at any team that thought it could get in our way. When Rutgers had tried to get to us in the regional semifinals, we'd pasted them, and started celebrating long before the game was over. Ace and I blew each other air kisses. I began to wonder if this was all too easy.

It was about to get harder. I felt like I was underwater in our next game, the regional final against North Carolina. There is no other way to describe it. I was out there on the court—same uniform, same shoes, same team, same everything, only I wasn't really there. My legs were so heavy. I couldn't do anything. As much as I tried, nothing was happening. The first half is like this blur. I'd get the ball, I'd shoot it, my shots would just . . . miss. I shot an air ball in the opening minutes. An air ball. I tried to do other things—defend, rebound—because I wasn't shooting at all.

They were pounding on me that night. I'd gotten used to that. Every team pounded on me, sending one, two, sometimes three players at me. I'd get bruised, I'd get sore, I'd get mad a lot too. That night, though, I felt like I was getting beaten. My arms ached, my back ached, and I knew when I took a shower later that there would be marks all over me. My teammates—especially the freshmen—were looking at me in shock. "Save us, Chamique!" is what their faces said. They hadn't been here before. I had. Two times. I was supposed to know what to do, how to fix things.

For some reason, though, I couldn't.

We were down by more than 10 points in the middle of the second half. I hadn't scored in so long I couldn't remember what it felt like to put the ball in the basket. Everything I shot missed. Everything. I remember my teammates played hard, trying to keep us close.

Whenever I had a bad game, Kyra would always rub my back and my shoulders in the huddle. She was there that night, rubbing and rubbing. She was supportive. She kept saying, "Mique! You've got the first half out of your system. Now you've got it, you've got it. I know you do."

When we finally started making some plays, the bench was crazy, jumping up and down, screaming for us. I started to get my game back. I made the basket that tied the game, I made the basket that finally put us ahead, and I made twelve of thirteen free throws down the stretch, when the Tar Heels finally got in trouble for the beating they'd been putting on me all night. But I felt lucky to have escaped that one with nothing more painful than scratches and bruises and a tremendous need to lay my body down on my bed and sleep. The season before, we wouldn't have survived a game like that, but now things were different. I had a supporting cast. If I couldn't get the job done—and there was a long, long stretch against Carolina when I couldn't—somebody else was going to figure out a way.

The Final Four was held in Kansas City that year. I still had my video camera, and was taping like mad. The semifinal game against Arkansas almost felt like a vacation after what we'd done the game before. We won by 28, even though I only shot 5-for-12 in the first half.

Louisiana Tech was our final opponent, and there was a lot of buildup. The word "dynasty" was being used all over the place, and the pressure certainly was on us to finish the season a perfect 39–0.

I'll never forget the first twelve minutes of that basketball game. There are people who say our team played the most perfect twelve minutes of basketball ever played in a women's college game. I read what they said about us in the newspapers afterward, and it was so flattering. They said I was relentless in the first few minutes. I drove through the lane with one, two, three defenders on me and still managed to score. I dropped in jumpers. If I missed, I got my own rebound and put it up again. I had 12 points before we'd played seven minutes, and 18 at halftime, with 7 rebounds. I don't know what happened. We were just so in control that night. The Louisiana Tech players looked glassy-eyed. We were so fast and athletic, and it definitely wasn't just me. Everybody on our team seemed to have the touch.

Coach Summitt took me out with about forty seconds to play, and though I'm usually humble, I admit I stuck three fingers in the air on my way off the court, to signal Three-Peat. Then I held up seven, to remind everyone that I'd won four in high school as well. It was out of character, and maybe I shouldn't have done that—I know it probably didn't make the players on Louisiana Tech feel good—but I was just so caught up in the moment.

After that, though, I calmed down. I hugged Coach Summitt, of course, and celebrated, but not the way I had the previous spring. My teammates—especially the freshmen—kept asking me why I wasn't more exuberant after we won that championship. "Mique, what's up? You're not very excited," they kept saying. It was true. I felt calm and relaxed, happy, but not crazy excited. Winning felt right, felt familiar by this point. I don't want to say I didn't appreciate that championship, because I did, but I would appreciate it a lot more after I learned what it felt like to lose the following spring.

Vice President Al Gore called the locker room that night to congratulate us and invite us back to the White House, where I'd already been the two previous years. Coach Summitt made sure I got on the phone.

I couldn't help myself. I had to tease him, even if he was the vice president of the United States.

"Aren't you going to get tired of seeing me at the White House?" I asked.

He laughed. At that point in my college career, I had so much faith in our team. I told reporters that night, "We're going to be even better next year." I didn't just want a fourth championship, I expected it. We weren't losing any of our starting five. In my heart,

I assumed that we would only get better. I was so naive then. I didn't know that things can change, and it can come back to really slap you in the face. I had to wait until the next season to learn that lesson, a hard lesson. A humbling lesson. That night, though, with everyone talking about our dynasty, it was easy to forget what my grandmother had always taught me about staying humble.

I announced that night that I was staying in school, but I kept getting asked the same question for the next few days. Everyone wanted to make sure that I hadn't made up my mind in the excitement of the moment. But I hadn't. I knew what I had to do.

"It's firm, it's final," I told reporters again and again. "I'm going to come back, be a better player next year, win another championship, and leave here in style."

Part of my decision was due to the lifelong influence of my grandmother, who would have been heartbroken if I'd left school without a degree. And part of it was Coach Summitt, who made it very clear to me that I now represented something special to a whole generation of young women and I had to be very, very careful about the example I set. If I left school early for the money, what kind of message would that be? The precedent I'd be setting would be a wrong one, an inappropriate one.

There was a point early in my career at Tennessee when I told Coach Summitt that I had no interest in being a role model. She just looked at me and said, "Tough, you already are, so you'd better figure out what kind of role model you want to be." It scared me at first when I ran out on the court and there would be all these little girls in Holdsclaw jerseys screaming for me. I'd sign autographs, and the kids would tell me, "I want to grow up to be just like you." That definitely makes you think.

So my decision to stay for my senior season was both personal and public. In my heart, I wanted to make my grandmother proud. And in my head, I knew that it was the right thing to do. Professional basketball could wait another year. If it was meant to be, it would happen. There was no reason for me to rush things. *Have a plan*, I always tell myself. And the truth was, all my life, my plan had been to get a college degree. I wasn't about to let the lure of a big contract and my own sneaker push me into throwing that plan away.

They held another parade for us when we got back to Knoxville Monday night, and I got my picture on the cover of the next week's *Sports Illustrated*. I was named the Naismith Player of the Year. Everyone in town was coming up to me, thanking me for the title. Life felt pretty good. But perfection never lasts long.

In the spring, after the season was over, I got a call in my room about my dad. As always, my family was trying to keep things from me so I wouldn't get too upset. They told me my dad was in trouble, that he wasn't okay. I was so thrown by the news that I don't even remember who it was that was on the other end of the phone. I thought there had been an accident, that he was hurt. My immediate reaction was *Oh my God! I've got to go see my father. I need to leave now.* But they didn't want me to come right away. They were trying to protect me.

My grandmother was the one who finally explained, or at least as much as she was willing to explain. She said my dad had had a nervous breakdown. That he'd been checked into Queens General to get some help, but he'd tried to get away. He wasn't stable. It was a really bad situation. She said he was under sedation, that they'd try to take care of him.

It crushed me to think about my dad in that situation. Through everything, he had tried so hard to stay close to me, to keep in touch, to know what was happening in my life. From the days in Jamaica when he used to come sit outside our building and wait to walk me to school in the morning, to the summer I was in college when he came and lived with me and my grandmother in our apartment so we could spend more time together, my dad was the one who always tried to hold our family together.

For a while, he'd gone back to South Carolina to be with his family. He'd send money back for Davon and me. But then he started drinking down there, and things weren't going so well. I blamed my mother then, wanted to know why she had always made my father look out for her when we were little but never paid attention to what help he might have needed, what problems he might have had. It wasn't fair, I know, but that's what I felt then.

My dad was put on medication, and for a while it seemed like every time I saw him he was glassy-eyed, out of it, not like he used to be. That was hard for me to see. For a long time, I struggled with that. My dad and I are so close, and now I have to be a grown-up and see him in a different light. See him as human, not just my dad.

He's better now, though. He's been sober for almost two years. He goes to a program. He lives in a home in Brooklyn and has people there to watch out for him. And he made it to my graduation from Tennessee, which touched me more than anything.

ZAKIYAH MODESTE ON CHAMIQUE

I met Chamique on campus our freshman year at Tennessee. Having grown up in New York with a dad who is a basketball referee, I knew all about her. I'd read her diary in the paper. I'd heard stories. But she wasn't at all what I expected.

We met at a party, I think, and since Chamique is from Queens, I was looking for this rough girl. Chamique was there with her roommate, Kim Smallwood, and Kim tends to be a little more hard-core than Chamique is—she has short hair, a more muscular build, she looks like an athlete. Chamique was just so thin, and all timid and quiet, like she is when she first meets someone. So when the two of them came into the room, I started talking to Kim, thinking she was Chamique. Once I got introduced, I was so surprised. This *is Chamique*? I thought.

Chamique never struck me as someone who came from the projects. I think she surprises a lot of people that way. People have their preconceptions. But she's a good girl who went to a Catholic school and had this great support system from her grandmother and her family. You see that in her.

She came out of her shell around me pretty quickly, but I could always sense her sizing up people. I was just friendly to everybody, but Chamique was more cautious. She knew she had to be careful, that certain people would want certain things from her. She was wise about that from the beginning. It was something she had to teach me.

Her life has changed so much since she left Tennessee, but we still talk to each other like it was yesterday. She's able to see both sides of life and knows how to stay in tune with the people who have been her friends and who helped her to get where she is. I know Chamique likes to talk about all the things I did for her—with her mail, and the fans, and everything—but I learned a lot from Mique too. She taught me patience. She taught me to have an open mind. She's always had both those things, and I think that's why she was able to just sit back and let things come to her at their own pace.

Chapter 9

*The "Three Meeks": Chamique, Semeka Randall,
and Tamika Catchings.*

wasn't prepared for how much crazier life was going to be when I returned to Tennessee my senior year. I'd always been a celebrity in Knoxville, with a lot of demands on my time. People would stop me on the street, in the mall, at dinner. It was a part of the life. I'd gotten used to it.

The year before, I had some great conversations about handling the public pressure of being an athlete in Knoxville with Peyton Manning, who was then a senior. If I thought I had it bad, well, Peyton had it ten times worse. Football is everything in Tennessee, and he was the best quarterback in the country. I thought the people in town were going to go insane when he didn't win the Heisman Trophy his senior year. It was a travesty in that town when that happened. A travesty.

Peyton and I liked to talk about how we dealt with our day-to-day lives in what was really a fishbowl. My advice to Peyton was that it took the same two seconds to be a jerk to somebody as it did to smile and sign the autograph, so why put in that negative effort? He was good about that, though. He was always respectful of the fans in Tennessee, and that's why people there still love him so much.

I think what you can never forget is how much responsibility comes with that kind of attention. It's more than just getting stopped for autographs or having people point at you in the mall and say, "Oh my God, that's Chamique Holdsclaw!" I can't count the number of times I've had little girls come up to me, crying. That's touching, really touching. It shocks you at first, that you can mean that much to someone you don't even know. I had to realize that I was in a position where what I did and what I stood for actually affected other people's lives.

When people come up to me and tell me that they respect what I stand for—my faith, my beliefs—it always makes me feel good. A lot of people tell me that they love my grandmother. I think my grandmother is a bigger hit in Tennessee than I am. People used to stop me on the street and ask, "When's your grandmother coming down again?" If she came to a game, there would be more people around her than around me.

To this day, I try my best not to let it get to be too much. Every night, I know when I step out of that locker room that there are going to be hundreds of kids there, lined up to get my autograph. So it doesn't matter how frustrated you are, or how mad, you just have to suck it up. You can't bring your attitude to someone else.

It's only because I've tried so hard to treat the fans right that I got so terribly upset the one time I was accused of blowing somebody off. There was a letter in a newspaper in Tennessee complaining that I had refused to sign an autograph after a game. I was so upset about that letter. I ranted about it to my roommate, Zakiyah. It just wasn't true. I had signed that night for at least twenty minutes, and then when I went back into the locker room, I think one of the security people must have stepped between me and someone else who was waiting. I don't know. But I never brushed people off like that. I always made sure I took the time to be good to the fans, and I really wanted people to know that, to know that I do appreciate their support. That even when my dinner gets interrupted or I'm trying to get out of the mall in five minutes, I never say no.

Coach Summitt was upset for me too. She knew how much public pressure there always is on me, and she knew how hard I had been trying to do the right thing. So in her next press conference, she went out of her way to address the issue and set the matter straight. I didn't ask her to, she just did. That meant a lot to me.

Peyton and I were both grateful, though, that we played for college programs that got so much attention, because that way we learned to deal with so many of the things that we'd have to deal with as pros. Take the media, for example. I was getting interviewed as early as high school, but being as shy as I am, it was never a really easy thing for me. I remember feeling awkward and a little silly talking to reporters when I first got to Tennessee, but by my senior year, I felt like an old pro. Of course, I also felt like I'd told the same stories about my life again and again and again. But the interest was only growing. By the time I made it to my senior spring, it was almost out of control.

In the meantime, though, I counted on friends like Zakiyah to keep me sane.

Zakiyah used to organize our shopping trips. She was a wonder. She'd keep a stash of Tennessee paraphernalia in our apartment—posters, cards, stickers, whatever. Whenever we needed to hit the mall, she'd grab a stack and make me autograph it before we left. I thought she was nuts. But she had a plan.

We'd go to the mall at 9:30 A.M., right after the stores opened, but that didn't matter. I always attracted attention. I'd be trying to do something simple, like buy socks, and it would take two hours. Everyone wanted to say hello, to shake my hand, to get an autograph. I was always polite, but it made it so hard to get anything done. I could never get in and out of anywhere: the mall, the grocery store, a restaurant. If I couldn't do my grocery shopping in the middle of the night, I'd send Zakiyah. She was good about stuff like that.

When people approached me in the mall, Zakiyah would smile, hand them a signed poster, and tell them, "Thanks! Here's an autograph. We're really in a hurry today." It was a nice compromise, because how can someone get angry when you're handing them an autographed poster? Sometimes they still wanted to stay and chat, but it certainly cut down on the delays.

Zakiyah looked out for my privacy in a lot of ways. We'd go out to dinner and without my knowing, she'd tell our waiter that I didn't want to be bothered during the meal, but I'd sign some things at the end. Usually, when I was in restaurants, people at other tables would ask their waiters to get something signed. Or someone who worked in the kitchen would come out to shake my hand. As I've said, I tried not to say no, ever, because the fans in Tennessee were so wonderful to me and I felt like I owed them some respect. I had one pet peeve, though. I hated it when people came over while I was eating and asked to shake my hand. I'm a very sanitary person, the kind who washes her hands before meals, and I didn't like shaking people's hands in the middle of my dinner. Call it one of my quirks.

Zakiyah was a blessing. She helped me a lot with my life, which was more than she needed to do. She would do little favors for me—pick something up, help me answer my fan mail. Whenever I asked, she'd always answer, "Mique, I got ya," but I'm sure it wasn't easy, living with me. For instance, even though our phone number was unlisted, we'd come home and there would be two dozen, three dozen messages on our answering machine. It was exhausting just to think about listening to all of them, but you never knew when there'd be one from a good friend or a family member buried somewhere in the middle.

Zakiyah's from New York, so we'd get together at home too, go shopping in Greenwich Village. We'd shop, shop, shop. She'd come over and hang out at my grandmother's apartment, take Davon with her to a party. Zakiyah's so much more New York than me—she moves fast, talks fast—and I'm always telling her to slow down, slow down. But ultimately, she's just so down-to-earth. And she knows how to snap me out of it when I get too caught up in things. She knows how to make me laugh. She's the biggest goofball I know.

Mostly, though, Zakiyah became one of those people I could trust. She's cool, but on point. And she knew me. She gave me my space, but I also came to see her as one of the few people in the world (like my grandmother) I didn't have to hide things from. She was the only person, besides Mickie, that I used to talk to about my frustrations about Coach Summitt. She listened and didn't judge. She's seen me cry my hardest—really bawl—and she's seen me act all crazy too. Since she was in my living space, she saw the things that I always hid from the public, and she knew how private I am. She used to joke when I walked out the door, "Got your game face on, Mique?"

I don't think I've ever worked as hard to get into shape as I did the summer after my junior year. I was dedicated. I played for the U.S. national team in the world championships in Berlin, and we won the gold medal. Then I went home to Astoria and hit the weights. I worked out every day. I played ball out on the middle park, and at the Boys and Girls Club. I wanted to take my game to another level. I was focused. I really believed that my senior year was going to be my best year. The team would only get better. I would only get better.

Maybe it was foolish of me to think that way. How can you be better than 39–0? But I believed it. In my heart, I believed it. And I knew it had to start with me. So I put in the hard work. I was dedicated. I wanted to accomplish the goal I'd set for myself the night we won the championship in Kansas City: I wanted to end my career in style. I wanted a fourth championship. What I didn't understand then, but I do now, is that these things aren't always under our control.

Little did I know at that time that I was due for the biggest disappointment of my basketball life.

LaShonda Stephens didn't come back that season, because her knees never recovered, but we had an incredible new recruit in Michelle Snow, a six-foot-five-inch freshman from Florida, so I didn't worry all that much. Besides, we had Kellie and we had the Meeks. What more did we need?

We started out that season with a loss in our second game, to Purdue. Purdue was going to be the national champion the next spring, but of course I couldn't know that then. I still believed we were the favorites.

As the season progressed, I may have developed some nagging suspicions we weren't as much of a team as we had been the year before—sometimes things just felt off, like people weren't as committed—but we did okay in the regular season and put together some amazing victories. I was still confident when we went into the postseason, even though we lost to Louisiana State in the final game of the regular season.

The pressure, though, was tremendous. After our junior season, people no longer just hoped we would win the title; they assumed we would. Everywhere I went, people talked about a fourth championship. I smiled when they said it. It was my dream, after all. And I had faith.

I was prepared for the end of my career at Tennessee, I just wasn't prepared for how it would end. The good-byes began in the second round of the NCAA Tournament, when I played what would be my last game at Thompson-Boling Arena. Of course, it was special to me. I played four years there. Just the fans there bring back incredible memories, because they were so supportive and so amazing. I hear the organ in my head. The band playing "Rocky Top." We always had a packed house. It was like home to me. There was this sense of belonging I'd get as soon as I stepped out on the court.

I was sad that last night. There was so much of my life that had taken place on that court. I wanted a great closing to what had been a great career. I thought about the fans all night—the fans, my teammates and, more than anything, just what being at Tennessee had meant for me.

I wanted to make my last game there a good one, and I did better than even I had hoped. We were playing Boston College, and I scored 39 points, to lead us to an 89–62 victory. It seemed like everything fell for me that night. Everything was perfect. When I came out of the game with a few minutes to play, I kissed the floor at the jump circle. It was something Kellie and I had planned, a way to say good-bye. She did the same.

The next weekend, we were off to Greensboro, North Carolina, for the regionals. The Final Four was to be played in San Jose, and all along I just figured we'd be there. Zakiyah had planned to come out for this Final Four, to hang out and have fun with me.

My family was coming. I was looking forward to it. Together, they'd take the edge off any pressure I might have been feeling.

Semeka was hurt that postseason, with two torn ligaments in her left ankle. She missed our games in Knoxville and barely got put together to go back on the court in Greensboro. But we didn't even need her all that much in the semifinal. We beat Virginia Tech, 89–62. Duke won the other semifinal. As always, I respected our opponent, but the Blue Devils didn't scare me. We'd beaten them before. And even with injuries, I thought we'd be able to beat them again.

Instead, it turned out to be the most difficult night of my career.

Duke was on fire. I wasn't. None of us were. My first ten shots missed. Front end, front end, front end. I kept putting the ball up, and I kept hearing the clank. I wasn't used to that sound. I kept thinking, *This time, it'll go in. This time, it'll be different.* It never got any different. By the time the game ended, I had shot a miserable 2-for-18 from the floor. I scored 8 lousy points. That tied my season low.

By halftime I was getting nervous, anxious, but after the comeback we'd managed to engineer against North Carolina the previous March, I knew better than to count us out of any game. I screamed at my teammates on the way out of the huddle, as much to wake myself up as to get a message to them. I was determined that one of us was going to step up, take charge. I wanted to be the one, but if I couldn't be, I had faith that someone else would do the job. I didn't know how to lose at this level. I wasn't about to start now.

Faith wasn't enough that night. Neither was determination. And with 25.4 seconds left on the clock and Duke in control, I fouled out. I was stunned, disbelieving. I walked to the side of the court and buried my head in Coach Summitt's shoulder. She was wearing a white blazer that night and I just wept on it, uncontrollably, apologizing for letting her down. I wanted to go in the locker room, leave, but Coach Summitt knew I needed to stay out there. She knew I needed to know how to lose.

She looked at me for a moment and said, "Chamique, you have

accomplished so much. Keep your head up." She sent me to sit down on the bench. I sat down next to Mickie, put a white towel over my face, and continued to cry. A few seconds later, Kellie got her fifth foul and came to sit on my other side, weeping just as hard as I was.

In all my years in basketball, I'd never been on the court when another team celebrated a championship. I didn't even know how to act. That loss, it took everything out of me. I'm not the type to sit there and just cry, but I did. I didn't know what else to do. They double-teamed me all the time. And my girls, Tamika and Semeka—it was like all of us had the worst game of our lives. Semeka's knee was hurt, Tamika was off. Nobody stepped up.

Since my junior year and the arrival of the Meeks, I felt confident that there was always somebody to step up if I didn't play well. Somebody else would be there. And it always happened. So when I look back at that game against Duke, it's just so hard to understand. None of us played well that night. The Three Meeks just did not perform. It was like we were invisible. It was something that had never happened before. Never. Kellie was carrying us offensively, and that's not really her job.

None of us had a great game. We didn't even have a good game. I have to believe everything happens for a reason, though. So I kept trying to figure out why—why?—did we lose like that. I'd sit back and think: *What was it? Did we think we were too good? Did we have too much arrogance? What did we do to deserve this?*

I was so dejected after that game. I was in the locker room, just crying, when my grandmother came in. She tried to console me. She's always been so good at consoling me. She told me that I had so much to be proud of and that this was only going to teach me a lesson, an important lesson. It was hard for me to listen to then. *What lesson?* I thought. *What lesson?*

All I could think about was how hard I had prepared in the off-season for this year, all the work in the weight room, all the time I spent on the court. I was thinking about how hard I'd worked during the season to improve my game, take it to another level. My grandmother told me to keep my head up, be proud. I knew she was right, but it wasn't easy. It took time.

129

* * *

When I got back to Tennessee, I was embarrassed. I would go out with black sunglasses on all the time. I didn't want anybody to say anything to me. I caught an attitude. All I wanted to do was finish the year, finish school.

So I moped for a while. It was hard not to. I'd never lost anything like that before. The whole time I was at Christ the King, we were always champions. Then at Tennessee, even during my difficult sophomore year, we won the title. So it really felt devastating to me to have it all end like that, without even making it past the regionals. And to play such a terrible game myself. Duke had outworked us. And I just wanted to hide.

Before I could hide, though, I still had to go to the Final Four with Coach Summitt. I had a banquet to attend, and I was supposed to play in an All-Star Game for some WNBA scouts. Coach Summitt knew it was going to be hard on me, so she sat me down the day after our loss—that Tuesday—and reminded me of everything we had accomplished in my four years at Tennessee and everything I still had to look forward to.

I'd finished my career with 3,025 points and 1,295 rebounds—both Tennessee records. We'd had a 131–17 record in my four years, which isn't bad, though I admit every one of those losses ached in my bones. I'd been named an All-American all four seasons, and Associated Press Player of the Year my last two years. Coach Summitt could have gone on listing things forever, but I wasn't ready to hear it. I appreciated the gesture, and tried to listen to what she said, but it was too soon. I wasn't ready to let go quite yet.

I was upset, but I had to be professional, so I did my best to keep my head up in San Jose. So many Tennessee fans were there that weekend—they'd booked trips assuming that we'd make it—and my family was there with me too. People kept coming up to me and saying, "You should be here, you should be here." My answer was always the same: "We didn't take care of business."

I didn't go to the games, and I really didn't want to play in the All-Star Game like I was scheduled. I almost backed out, but Kellie said she was going to play, so I told them I would play on Kellie's team. It was like our way of saying good-bye to each other. We needed that one last time on the court together, because it had ended so abruptly for us.

After I made it through Final Four weekend, I returned to campus and went into semiseclusion. Zakiyah had never seen me so down. I didn't want to go out, didn't want to talk to anybody. It's not that I thought people were going to blame me—actually, people were so supportive it was overwhelming. They sent flowers to my apartment, sent me letters, kind notes. One of the letters I received was from Peyton, who told me to keep my head up, then offered any assistance he could when it came to dealing with things on a professional level. That letter touched me, so I did call him, and we talked a few times that spring. He was already with the Indianapolis Colts then, but he still had time to help me.

No matter how many letters or calls of support I received, though, I still blamed myself for our loss. For a while, I felt as if the loss was all my fault, that I was the one who was supposed to have stepped up, and by not doing that, I'd let all my teammates down, I'd let the fans down, I'd let so many people down. It didn't help that I became the first female basketball player to win the Sullivan Award, which is given to an outstanding college athlete. That wasn't what I was about—the individual achievements. I had wanted the championship. It's the only award that mattered to me.

Not wanting to lose is what had always motivated me. Not wanting to taste defeat. I hated to lose, and I had done it so infrequently. I already had three championships, and I thought I could draw on my competitive fire in that last game. In my head, I was thinking, *They want to take this from me, and I'm not going to let them.*

What bothered me most was that I felt like we hadn't lost from a talent perspective, we'd lost from a mental perspective. Our team didn't come to play every game. We had mental lapses. Some people didn't show up sometimes. It was crazy. It wasn't like the year before. Coach Summitt got so frustrated. She kept saying, "I can't play *for* you."

Why was our team so different from one year to the next? I don't know why. I don't think I'll ever know why. I could kill myself trying to figure out, but after a while I just had to let it go.

It took me at least a few weeks to realize that what my grandmother and Coach Summitt were telling me was true. I had to accept that it was a blessing, what I'd accomplished. I'd had a great collegiate career. We won three consecutive national championships, set a precedent that, hopefully, will give somebody else something to shoot for. So how could I feel sad?

I had a family that was so proud of me, I was about to get my degree, the WNBA draft was around the corner. The Lord had blessed me. I had so much, I didn't want to be spoiled and just complain and complain and be unappreciative of everything good that had happened. It hurt, but it was only a game. I had to remember that: it was only a game.

I've succeeded a lot in my life, so if I fail a couple of times, that has to be okay. It's about building character. Coach Summitt told me I would learn more from that one loss than anything else that had happened to me at Tennessee, and she was right. I guess God wanted to teach me how to handle failure. I wasn't supposed to sit there and question what happened, I needed to accept that it was meant to be. It was a lesson that was going to be so valuable to me in the future—in the WNBA, where I was about to learn a whole lot more about losing, and in life, where I think I'd always known that no matter how hard you plan, things don't always work out your way.

LON BABBY ON CHAMIQUE

I know exactly when it dawned on me that Chamique was going to be at a different level than women athletes who had come before her. It was the day we went to Nike headquarters in Oregon for contract negotiations. At the time, there was a war between Nike and its competitors for Chamique's services. She had just finished college, hadn't started playing for the Mystics yet.

When we arrived, there was a big Chamique Holdsclaw banner over the entrance. A huge banner. I represent a lot of male athletes, so I know this is something that Nike does often, but it still made an impression. Nike also had Chamique Holdsclaw T-shirts with all of her accomplishments listed on the back. They were incredibly well prepared. We went from department to department, and she got as strong a recruiting pitch at Nike as any I'd ever seen. She even met Phil Knight. For me, that Nike trip was the first time I really appreciated the extent to which Chamique was at a level with the real superstars on the men's side of the game. There was no appreciable difference between the treatment Tim Duncan received by Nike and the treatment Chamique received. I thought that was extraordinary. It seemed to me that Nike was showing its understanding of her importance to the evolution of the women's market.

What has really been a joy to watch, though, has been the way in which Chamique has handled all this attention. A lot of great female athletes have gotten women to this point and now Chamique is climbing the steps to the top. I know she's aware of it and I know she's aware of the responsibility that brings, but she's handled it with admirable grace and humility.

Chapter 10

*Chamique both inspires and draws
strength from the children she meets.
Pictured here with her friends and fans
from Astoria.*

My last few months at Tennessee were truly crazy. I had to finish classes, take my exams, get ready to graduate. But that was the simple part. The WNBA draft was looming. I had been named to the U.S.A. women's basketball team again, and I had responsibilities to them. First, though, I needed to sign with an agent, as quickly as possible. It was time to figure out my future. And that was an overwhelming task.

Picking an agent or a lawyer to represent me was a little bit daunting. It's such a big decision—these are the people you are going to trust to take care of you, to advise you on what is best, to make sure you get the right contracts and work with the right people. And it's not like I had any experience in all of this.

To be honest, I was really naive about agents when I was at Tennessee. Agents have been hanging around and chasing after male athletes forever—you're going to see them all over Knoxville after football season is over, with the guys we have playing there—but it wasn't something that women ever had to deal with before the WNBA and the ABL. Coach Summitt and I talked about that. Mickie too. All of a sudden they had to worry about rules violations and illegal contact and these issues that had never been a part of the women's game before. It worried them. And I was definitely at the middle of all that, because I was probably the first woman player anybody ever talked about as possibly going pro before finishing college.

It was amazing how hard so many agents tried to get to me. They called Zakiyah's and my apartment, even though our number was unlisted. They called my house in Astoria. They'd even get some of the football players I knew at Tennessee to pass along their numbers, urging me to call them. Thank goodness my grandmother is a smart woman. She'd talk to some of them when they called the house, but she kept them away from me. I had nothing to do with it.

There's one story that Coach Summitt likes to tell as a warning to her players now, about this woman lawyer who pretty much pretended to be my friend in order to get close to me. She used to call my dorm room sophomore year, say she was looking for my roommate, then she'd just talk and talk to me. Like Mickie always says, I'm much more relaxed and friendlier on the phone. So I'd talk to her. Then one time we're out of town and she approached me in person, wanted to go back to my room and hang out. She's a thirty-year-old lawyer and I'm this college kid and maybe I was just so naive, but it didn't register, until Mickie interfered, that this woman was just trying to get to me and use me. When that kind of thing happened, though, it only made me realize how important it was that I pick an agent I could trust.

Tennessee did a really great job for me, though, as far as keeping track of things my junior and senior years, when the mail started coming from different agents. They had a compliance officer review it, and then I'd get a list. She'd tell me, "Chamique, this is who you've gotten mail from." I'd read the list, sort through it. And after my senior season was over, they gave me the mail and I started looking.

I got advice from a lot of people—from Coach Summitt, from Peyton Manning, who had been taken number one in the NFL draft the year before, so he certainly knew what I was going through. I talked to Lisa Leslie and Nikki McCray a little bit. Coach Summitt even talked to Peyton's dad, who was great.

I figured out that what I needed was somebody who was known, who had ties with all the different marketing companies, who was high profile. And I needed somebody I felt comfortable with. But what I really wanted was to get the whole process over with as quickly as I could.

I met with four different groups. They all flew down to Tennessee to see me. I decided on Lon Babby and his associate Jim Tanner from Williams & Connolly for a lot of reasons. I didn't really know that much about them at first, but they seemed very professional, and I liked that they were an established firm with clients like Grant Hill, Tim Duncan, Jerome Williams, Nykesha Sales. That's the kind of company you'd like to keep. Lon is a lawyer, not an agent, and I pay him by the hour, rather than a commission, which so many agents today want. Sometimes they want as much as 20 percent of your endorsement contracts. There are some people who need their agents to go out there and really work to bring them those things, but I've been pretty blessed, and they just kind of come. So I wanted somebody like Lon, who I thought was really professional, and I just hit it off with Jim too, right away. They were based in D.C., which seemed like a good thing, since the Mystics had the first pick in the draft, and that's where I was likely to end up.

I tried to be humble when people kept telling me that I was the sure number-one pick in the draft, even though the ABL had folded and so many veteran players were going to be available in addition to those of us coming out of college. Everyone seemed to want me to end up in New York, playing for my hometown Liberty. I didn't think it would be a bad thing to be in Washington. I worried about the distractions in New York, to be honest. When I went to play in Madison Square Garden when I was still in college, my cell phone was ringing and ringing—even in the locker room, on game day—with people who knew me from the old neighborhood or high school or whatever who wanted tickets, who wanted to say hello, who wanted to hang out. It was overwhelming. And I knew it would just get worse if I ended up there professionally, at least right away.

I was even worried a little bit about Washington, about being close enough for people to drive in for games, about having to worry about houseguests all the time while I'm trying to concentrate on playing for the team. Already I could see that there were going to be a lot of responsibilities in my life. That much became clear before I even finished school.

At Tennessee, Coach Summitt and everyone guarded me pretty well. I was sheltered from a lot of the craziness that comes along with being a well-known athlete, even if I did get a lot of attention at the grocery store or the mall. Now I was in the real world. They wanted me in Los Angeles to tape an episode of the HBO show *Arliss* one week. I also had an obligation with the U.S.A. team to meet in Hawaii. I had all kinds of interview requests, and it wasn't just the guy next door anymore. These were big things, and the whole time I'm still in school, I've got academics, I've got to go to class. I grew up to another level really quickly because I had no choice but to focus.

Then draft day came. May 4. I had two exams I was supposed to take just two days later at Tennessee, to finish my degree in political science and public administration. I couldn't concentrate on that at all, though. We were all in a room at Madison Square Garden— me, Natalie Williams, Yolanda Griffith, DeLisha Milton, some other players who were expected to go near the top of the draft. I was saying, "Who is going to go first?" and everyone kept telling me, "Mique, you *know* you're going to Washington." And that's when I made a really, really stupid mistake. I don't bite my tongue or say things without thinking that much, but some reporter asked me, "How would you feel about getting drafted first and going to Washington?" and I answered, "I'd be excited with anything, as long as I don't go to Utah." It was stupid, and it insulted everyone in Utah, and now whenever I go to Utah, I get booed. I feel so bad about that.

There was a ton of press on draft day. It was kind of crazy. I had to do a signing at the NBA store in midtown Manhattan and I remember Mystics president Wes Unseld and Coach Nancy Darsch calling me up on the phone while I was there. They said they were excited to have me, and we talked for a while. My grandmother was there with me, and the rest of my family.

It's hard to describe what it's like getting drafted. When it happens, you just think, *Wow*. It doesn't really hit you until later on. It probably didn't hit me until about a week later, when I'm thinking, *Dag! For once, I'm really going to get to play close to home. My family's going to get to see me. How is this going to be? How am I going to handle everything?*

We never talk about basketball much when I'm around my family. My grandmother is more concerned with how I am as a person. It's the same with some of my old friends. They'd pay attention to what was going on at Tennessee and say things sometimes, but basketball wasn't what they cared about. I wondered if that would change. I wondered if it would be stressful—my friends able to just drop in and come see me play. My family in town a lot. Having to entertain people. I've never been all that good about having people I know in the stands. Even when I got my grandmother tickets and she came to games at Tennessee, I never wanted to know where she was sitting. It was just easier for me that way.

So I was wondering about how to handle this new stage in my life. Did I want my family to visit all the time? Did I want Anthony and Cheron to hang with me initially, or did I want to wait until I got acclimated to my new environment? Did I want my grandmother to come down as much as she could and stay with me? Or was I going to try to do this alone first to see how it was? That's what I was thinking: *What am I going to do? How is my life going to be now?*

You know when it really hit me? When I was back at Tennessee after the draft and they had a press conference for me and Kellie Jolly—who got taken in the fourth round by Cleveland—and all the reporters who had been watching my career the whole time at Tennessee were talking about how I had made number one. It just sunk in then. It was like I realized, right at that moment, that there was no more Tennessee for me, that this is a whole new thing. And to be honest, we were talking about how the Mystics were a terrible team and the reporters wanted to know if I could turn it around and make things better. And all of a sudden I'm thinking, *Dag! This is going to be pressure.*

First, though, I had to get through the last few days of school:

138

exams, graduation, Kellie's wedding, where I was supposed to be a bridesmaid.

We graduated in Thompson-Boling Arena, which seemed kind of suitable to me. All my years at Tennessee, that had been the place where I'd had so many important moments, and when I walked across the stage and got my diploma, I was proud. My grandmother had wanted me to earn that degree more than she had wanted anything, and it meant everything in the world to me to show her that I had. My father was there too, and after what he'd been through in the last year, it was really emotional for me to see him come. Things were straightening out for me. He almost looked like the dad I remembered from when I was young.

I still want to kill Kellie for keeping me from going out to eat with my family after graduation—I had to go to her wedding rehearsal instead, because she was getting married the very next day. So I only took a few minutes to see my grandmother and my parents and Davon before getting in my car and heading for Kellie's house, which was a few hours away in Sparta.

I'd never been in a wedding before, and this one seemed perfect—sweet, but funny too. Kellie would look at me and the other bridesmaids with this face that made it so hard not to laugh. But her husband, Jonathan Harper, he was this great guy, a superperson, and I could see how happy she was. I knew this was what she wanted. I was happy for them.

That day was crazy, because I was supposed to be in Washington for practice the very next afternoon, and so I had to say so many good-byes. Kellie, of course, and the whole team were there, and Coach Summitt. It was late, dark, when I got into my car and headed back to school. Then I packed up and started the ten-hour drive to Washington, ready to start my new life.

I don't think I was prepared for how many demands there were going to be on me when I started camp for the Mystics, and how quickly it all would come. There were meetings, interviews, tons of people there every day after practice. Public appearances all the time. Photo shoots. *Good Morning America* following me around for a week. Moving to a new city, everything. That was tough. That's the part that shocked me the most, I guess. Even after Tennessee and all the attention and pressure you have in that program, I wasn't prepared for what this would be like. It was so much at one time. If it had just been the media, like I'd dealt with at Tennessee, I would have been okay. If it had just been moving to a new city and finding a new place to live, I could muster that. But it was—boom!—everything. It was moving into a house, shopping for furniture, picking out stuff, scheduling interviews, answering a hundred questions. I'm new in town and I go out and all I do is walk down the street and people are yelling, "Chamique! Chamique!" All of this, and I was only twenty-one years old.

For the first week or so of training camp, I lived in a hotel where several of my teammates were staying because my town house wasn't ready. Finding a place had been a whirlwind for me. I'd come to Washington the day after the draft to meet with the organization, and my lawyers asked me then where I wanted to live. I'd decided on northern Virginia, because I liked that area, and I'd decided I wanted to rent a town house. So my lawyers found a broker who showed me two or three places, and then I essentially had two days to make up my mind. In other words, I didn't spend much time finding my new home. I didn't have the time, honestly.

I ended up with a three-bedroom town house in Alexandria. When I first moved in, I picked out a few of the necessary things—furniture and stuff—but to be honest, to this day I haven't had time to really decorate. My life is still crazy most of the time. But it was the worst for me those first few weeks in D.C.—I was just starting to get used to having such a demanding schedule. Then, when everything seemed to hit me all at once, I'd go home, so tired from practice, ready to just take a break, and then I'd remember something else, like my family was coming to visit and I didn't have enough beds yet, so I had to go out and buy beds. And through all of this, what I wanted to do was get to know my teammates, get comfortable in this new place, and it just didn't seem like there were enough hours in the day.

Even my days off were crazy. It was an unbelievably sunny spring morning when I met up with Nicole Hawkins, a media relations person for the Mystics, to make one of the many public appearances I've promised to make. This was one of those rare—really rare—days when Coach Darsch gave us a day off from practice, and there was so much I needed to do. My town house was in desperate need of more furniture—not to mention sheets, towels, kitchenware, all those little things—and I still didn't know my way around Washington all that well. I needed to call my brother, Davon, check in with my grandmother, run errands.

It's hard for me to say no, though, when they ask me to make public appearances, and it really is my responsibility to be available for things like this. This is when I get the most nervous, and the most shy—when I have to speak in front of five thousand people or do some big appearance. It's been one of the hardest things for me, getting past my shyness in these kinds of situations. Even now, after I've been doing it for years, I still get butterflies in my stomach.

I remember the first time I had to give a speech in front of a bunch of people—I was only seventeen, a senior in high school, and I had won the Naismith Award for player of the year in high school, and they were giving it to me at a banquet in Atlanta. It was the year Rebecca Lobo was player of the year for women in college, and Joe Smith was player of the year for the men. I was supposed to give a speech in front of thousands of people and I practiced and practiced and practiced. I was terrified, but when I went up there, it was almost easy, and everyone said I did a great job. It's always like that for me—I'm so nervous and scared, then once I get started, it's almost a breeze. I pretty much have a plan for all my speeches. When I talk to adults, they like to hear about my grandmother and the focus she gave me, and they're interested in what it takes to succeed as a team and how we did that at Tennessee. Businesses even have me make little videos to give to their workforce sometimes, where I talk about leadership and teamwork and the sacrifices you have to make if you want to reach your goals.

Anyway, on this particular May morning, I was scheduled to appear at Hardy Middle School in northwest Washington. A crew from ESPN was coming, and they were taping a question-and-answer session with the kids for a series they air on professional athletes in the community. The school felt like any middle school—the long, dim locker-lined hallways, the signs hanging on the walls. Talking to kids is the most fun, but it also can be the most stressful. Kids are so honest. They ask you the most unbelievable questions. They'll just walk up to you and say things like, "Why are you wearing *that* shirt?" They can be blunt and silly, wanting to know how much money you make or what kind of car you drive. And then they can be so serious, pushing you to talk about drugs or peer pressure—or even your love life—with none of the embarrassment adults seem to have. They're little kids, and they just call it as they see it, and I think that's kind of fun. That's why I like working with them the most, because I can joke with them, rag on them a little, and they just laugh and enjoy it.

I don't give structured speeches to the kids. I just know what I want to stress and write down four or five points, and then just talk, talk to them, answer their questions. I almost always talk about the value of working hard and what it can earn you, because that is something I learned from my grandmother and something that's definitely been true in my life. What I say also depends on the situation. I think I can relate to kids from all different backgrounds and environments because of my experiences. There are kids from broken homes everywhere—in poor neighborhoods, in middle-class neighborhoods, from rich neighborhoods. The same goes for girls who want to grow up to be athletes and are looking for role models to encourage them and make them believe that anything is possible.

I have to admit, though, I feel a special bond when I talk to kids who come from the inner city like I did. I understand some of the things they are dealing with that other kids don't face, and it's my passion to make them believe that hard work can get you anywhere, no matter where you come from. I'm living proof of that, so I really feel it in my heart when I see those kids with all their hopes and dreams.

That day at the middle school, I didn't really prepare much, because the ESPN format was supposed to have the kids asking most of the questions. But I admit that getting filmed at the same time made me a little more nervous.

I remember I was wearing a Donna Karan outfit—thin white pants, a pink knit top, a blue linen shirt. I was so excited about that outfit. Maybe some professional athletes take for granted all the things people want to do for them and give them now that they have a Nike shoe or a commercial, but I'm new enough to this that when I walked into the DKNY store in New York City and the manager told me they wanted to dress me, I was really flattered.

A woman came up in the hall to greet me while the ESPN crew was setting up inside. She worked for the school, I think, and she was telling me that she knows someone I know and had even met me once before, and I tried so hard to remember, but it's hard. This happens to me all the time—people make these connections to you, and you don't want to hurt anyone by admitting you don't know what they are talking about or you don't remember, but a lot of the time you really don't. I meet so many people, shake so many hands, sign so many autographs. It's impossible to keep everything straight.

Once it was time to go into the classroom, a member of the crew clipped a mike to my shirt, and nervousness struck again. I could hear the kids in the classroom—it was Betty Brown's room 101, according to the little sign by the door—giggling and talking. They wanted me to make an entrance, so I did, not sure what I was going to say when I got up there. But the kids burst into applause, and then I was looking out at those faces, all these sixth- and seventh- and eighth-graders, so eager, so excited, and as always, it wasn't as hard as I thought it was going to be.

"Chamique! Chamique! Who was the most important person in your life?" The question came from a boy wearing a blue T-shirt.

"My grandmother," I answered. That one was easy. I can talk about Grandma forever.

I answered questions about my car (a Lexus SUV) and the Mystics and Tennessee, and laughed when one kid wanted to know if I live in a mansion.

"No, no mansion," I said. "I'm not big-time yet. I live in a town house."

Afterward, they asked me to go into the gym and take a picture, and all of a sudden the kids were clamoring for me to stay, to play ball with them, and I wanted to, but I had another appearance to make—a place I had to be in less than an hour—and so I had to say no. That's the hardest part of this job, saying no like that. So I promised to come back another day. Maybe I shouldn't make promises like that so easily, because with the team and our travel schedule and all the other responsibilities I have, it's rare that I have a free day, or even a free morning. But there I was, promising anyway. "If I don't come back," I joked with the kids, "you guys can talk about me like, 'That Holdsclaw! She lies!'"

The kids loved that. And I meant it. But as soon as we got out of the room, I made Nicole Hawkins promise me that she'd get somebody to put it on my schedule. Or at least try. I live by my schedule now, and most of the time I don't even know what's on it until I'm told. That's a part of my life now, all these responsibilities I have to different people.

Nicole told me that I didn't have much time, that school let out in a few weeks and it probably wouldn't be able to happen.

"Just give me directions," I told her. "I'll drive myself up here after practice one day."

I'm sorry to say, I never did. But I really meant what I said to those kids about how they should hold me accountable. It's like my grandmother always telling me to stay humble. That's important. It's so gratifying to me when reporters talk to my friends from home and my friends from Tennessee and they always say that I haven't changed since my life changed and that I'm still "just Chamique."

Of course, things are different. They have to be. First of all, there is the money. As soon as I was officially signed with an agent, the contracts started rolling in. For Nike. For Nickelodeon. For Gatorade. Eventually, for the Mystics and the WNBA. It was pretty incredible. I've never felt like I've really wanted for anything important in my life, but all of a sudden, here I was in a position where I was earning more money than I'd ever thought about in my life. I had people I was paying to work for *me*. I had to pay people salaries. It was exciting, but the most important part was being able to feel like I could help my family, no matter what happened or what they needed. If my grandmother needs something, I can take care of her. And my brother too. My whole family. I helped my mom get her new house in Westchester. I would buy my grandmother a new place, but she refuses. In fact, she never even wanted to know how much money I was making. All she wanted to do was lecture me about money sometimes changing people and how she hopes that doesn't happen to me. She reminded me about the "real world" as she calls it, like our little world in Astoria wasn't real.

"You have to stay humble, Chamique," she told me for the millionth time.

And I answered the same way I always do. "Oh, Grandma," I said, "you know I'm okay." I sighed really loudly, teasing her. But I was listening. When it comes to my grandmother, I always do.

So when I do spend my money, I really do try to be careful. I've always been a shopper, so it could get dangerous. I got myself some of the things I've always wanted—a big screen television, a DVD player, and a surround sound system. But I'm not one of those people to go out and waste money on things that are extravagant. I'm kind of conservative about those things. People speculate on how much money I make all the time, but I always say to myself, *I don't care how much money I have—I don't care if people say I'm making the most of any woman player ever—I just want to make sure I have something to show for it.* I'm not going to bank on playing basketball for ten years. While I have this money now, I'm going to save and invest it. I'll buy some things, because I've worked for this. I've worked to have certain nice things. But for me that means nice clothes, or a nice watch, not four cars and some mansion on a hill. It's like the Mercedes-Benz S-500 I saw. Of course, I wanted it. I thought about buying it for days. But deep down, I felt like I was too young to be spending money on a car like that. I don't deserve something like that. I'm not old enough to appreciate it yet.

What I decided to do was have a financial adviser who would put me on a budget. Basically I said, here, I signed this contract, and this is what I want to have in the bank at the end for security.

Put me on a budget that tells me how much I can spend each month and still save enough to reach the goal I'm aiming for. So he did that, and that was the end of it.

As far as money goes, I've been lucky when it comes to my family. You read and hear about all these professional athletes whose entire families are living off what they make and who expect so much from them and have all these demands, and my family hasn't been like that. They know I'm willing to help out, but it's not like they are coming to me asking for things all the time. My family's not like that. My brother jokes about things, saying I have to get him a car, but he knows what my rules are. I make sure he has money for school and for clothes and things—he's at that age, you know, where he has to be stylish. That's important. But I tell him he can't have a car until he gets through a year of college and I see first if he deserves it.

Actually, my brother was the first one to tell me, "I don't want anything from you," even though people are always going around saying things to him about "your sister" this and "your sister" that. But Davon says I should be living my life for *me*. He calls me sometimes for little things, like he knows I can get him the new Jordans first, but the way he asks me is always so respectful. And my answer is always the same: "How are you doing in school? How are those grades?"

Sometimes it seems like Davon has gotten so independent, and it's easy for me to not call for a while or let things slide. But then there's always something to remind me that he's still my little brother, no matter how much he's grown up.

There was this one day, near the beginning of my first season in Washington, when Davon called me, teasing, and pretended to be a stranger.

"May I speak to Chamique Holdsclaw, please?" he asked.

"Davon!" I said. "You know it's me!"

He was mad at me for not calling enough. I knew it. It's hard for Davon to understand why I'm too busy to check in as often as I should, and I admit that it's something I need to be better about.

I was reading *USA Today* one day and I saw a little item about Michael Jordan, and how his sister gave an interview to some television station and accused him of not caring about his mom and not going to visit and not keeping in touch with his family. And I'm not saying I believe it just because she said it, but all I could think is: *I don't ever want my family to say that about me.* When you come home to your apartment and there are twenty-nine messages on your voice mail—and your number is unlisted—it's hard to keep in touch with all the people who are expecting things of you, but my family needs to come first. Davon is so important to me, and I know I have to do better. I still feel like it's my job to watch over him. My grandmother told me that his guidance counselor is worried about him, that he misses me and people can see that. It makes me feel terrible. So much of my life I've tried to look out for Davon, to make things easier for him, going all the way back to when he was little and I took the fifty dollars to buy him that G.I. Joe. So it's even harder for me to accept that being who I am has made things difficult on Davon. Of course, he's proud of me. I know that. But I can understand how frustrating it must be to play basketball and have everyone compare you to your famous big sister. To always hear people say, "Why aren't you as good as Chamique? Why aren't you as tall as Chamique?" If I could make that stop, I would. But I can't protect him from everything.

When he comes to visit me now, or I go home and see him, it always shocks me to see how grown-up he's become. I always think of him as my little tagalong, and I suppose I always will. But he's becoming a man now, going off to college this fall, and I can't watch over him the way I used to. If nothing else, I don't have the time. If there's anything I learned my first year as a pro, it's how precious time has become.

CHERON SCALES ON CHAMIQUE

One thing about Chamique and me: we always used to like to leave the projects, to go off on adventures. We'd go to New Jersey to go shopping. We'd go into the city. We'd go to SoHo. We were just teenagers—we've been friends forever—and we'd go anywhere, just to do something different. Mostly, they were just these little trips out of our neighborhood, but I'm grateful for them. It opened your eyes, I think.

In the projects, it's easy to get involved with the wrong things. Sometimes it's like a chain reaction: kids stay there, don't ever get motivated to leave, and just fall into things. I thank God that never happened to me, and I knew it was never going to happen to Chamique.

Still, I know when Chamique does come back to New York that she likes to go back to Astoria. She feels like she has a place there, and it's special for her. In that way, she hasn't changed. She's still so humble. It's a cliché, I guess, to say that success hasn't changed a person, but that's true of Chamique. I've known her for so long, and it's still the same with us, and with everyone she loves in her life. Chamique cares so much about her friends and her family. I used to watch her with Miss June, the way they'd joke with each other and tease each other, and it was obvious how much they really love each other. I'd watch her with Davon too. They had a real brother-sister relationship—always fighting, even though they were so close.

She's just as close to all of them, now, and just as close to me and Anthony and her friends. She's still a clown. She still thinks she can rap, when we all know she can't. I can remember sitting with her in McDonald's, having her ask me to kick a beat on the table so she could rap: "Sitting in McDonald's / Me and Cheron / Just got done shopping . . ." We'd all laugh so hard. That's the thing about Chamique: when you really know her, she's the best. I love her. I do.

Chapter 11

Chamique with fellow Mystic Nikki McCray in Italy.

Staying in Tennessee for my graduation and Kellie's wedding made me two days late for my first training camp. No one seemed to mind. The fans had been terrific when I'd come to D.C. to visit a week after the draft. The organization held a welcoming party for me at Union Station, and all these people came out to meet me. In a city where the Wizards have struggled badly, I think people were excited to have someone with a winning track record arrive.

Right away, I had a comfort zone at practice because there were so many familiar faces. I knew Muriel Page from having played against her so many times. Nikki McCray was a Tennessee graduate, and even if our time hadn't overlapped, I'd heard a lot about her from Coach Summitt.

And there was Rita Williams, who became one of my closest confidantes almost immediately. I called her before I even got to camp because she wore my number—number 23—and I knew that because she was a veteran, the team was not going to make her give it up. But I wanted that number. It's special to me. I can't imagine playing without it.

Rita and I knew each other because of all the times Tennessee played Connecticut—she graduated from UConn—but it's not like we knew each other that well. Still, when I called her that first day, we were on the phone for almost an hour and a half, just talking, before I even asked for the number. I felt a little bad about it, and I just said, "Um, well, um, I'd really like to wear number twenty-three. I don't know if you want me to pay you for it or whatever, but it's important to me."

Rita was great. She said, "Look, I'm a nice person. I'm cool. If you want the number, you can have it." She didn't even want anything for it. But I know it's customary in pro sports for a rookie to pay up if he or she takes somebody else's number, so I had a special set of golf clubs made for her, with her name on them. She liked that.

Once I got to camp, though, and we realized we were so much alike, we really hit it off. Our personalities are very similar. Rita is quiet, like I am, and like most of my close friends. She's laid-back. I'm laid-back. She's also very analytical. And she listens. I didn't know during those first few weeks how important it was going to be for me to have a friend on the team who was there to listen and analyze during the difficult season that was to come. Rita turned out to be that person, and for that, I'm so grateful. At that point, though, it was just nice to have a friend.

Camp was tough, I guess, but not after the discipline of playing in Coach Summitt's system. I was surprised too, by the attitude. I thought things would be different in the pros. To me, this was a job. I assumed that I had to show up at camp in excellent shape. And that everyone else would too. Instead, I got there and we were doing all these conditioning and training workouts that are supposed to get us *into* shape. I admit, it annoyed me. When you have a job, you should show up prepared, and your coaches should expect that. At least, that's how I see it. We always showed up prepared at Tennessee. It seemed to me that Tennessee had been far more professional, but I tried not to make a comparison. One of the hard things about coming from a successful program like Tennessee—and playing for a great coach like Pat Summitt—is that you find yourself disappointed when you try to compare other things to that. It's a problem that I struggled with all year.

* * *

I tried not to let myself be daunted by the incredible expectations that swirled around me from the moment I was taken first in the draft. It was more than a hope that I'd turn things around for the Mystics. I was supposed to be the new centerpiece of the WNBA, at a time when the league was still young and growing, and trying so hard to capture the country's interest. My lawyer, Lon Babby, explained it pretty well. "Chamique is coming of age at the same time that women's basketball is coming of age, and she's going to be expected to do more than just play well," Lon told a reporter at the start of the season. "She'll be expected to help grow the league, and I think people hope she'll be the wave that people can ride as this sport continues to move into the future. They want everything from her. They want her to transcend even basketball and become a spokesperson and a public figure who represents the evolution of women's sports overall."

How's that for pressure?

My reaction, as always, was to focus on basketball and try not to get too caught up in the hype. It was impossible, though, to be oblivious to the fact that everyone was talking about me like I was going to have this huge immediate impact, both on the Mystics and on the league. How could I avoid it when I was getting asked about it almost every day? I also knew it was bothering other players, but I couldn't do anything about that.

During preseason, we played the Houston Comets in Knoxville, in a game designed to be a homecoming for me. I was so excited. It was like a little pro debut for me—playing the two-time WNBA champions in front of my Tennessee fans. That night, Sheryl Swoopes and Cynthia Cooper, two of the best players in the league, were grabbing on me and pushing me and letting me know that everybody was going to be rough on me at this new level, which is fair, and what I expected. We won, though, and I felt like it was a big step for me and an even bigger step for the organization. It was definitely something for the organization to draw upon. It brought some excitement to the Mystics.

Afterward, I heard that Sheryl complained to reporters about how she was sick of hearing nothing but "Chamique, Chamique,

Chamique." I was prepared for something like that, because Coach Summitt had warned me that some players would be resentful of the attention I'd be getting. I didn't say anything, because it's not like I have anything against Sheryl, and I felt like the media tried to blow it out of proportion. I don't think she really felt like they made her out to feel.

This is the way I see it: God devises everyone's plans in life. No matter how much people might be against you, they can't block your blessings, because they're meant to be. I truly believe that. So when I hear about that, I think: *To each his own. Don't get on me because something happens to me and I end up in a position you don't like. Remember, I didn't ask for it. I worked for it. And it's not something I could control.* I couldn't control the attention—it's not like I asked *Good Morning America* to follow me around Washington—and I couldn't control the way other players in the league felt about it. So I just had to let it go.

I can never understand, though, why women in competitive fields always act like there's not enough to go around, and why instead of being supportive of one another, they try to knock one another down. When we break through in a field that's dominated by men—like we're doing in basketball—you'd hope that the women who make the breakthroughs would be excited and inspired by the women who are coming up after them. That's what pushes you, after all, the competition of knowing someone else is right there at your feet.

For some reason, though, women don't seem to look at it that way a lot of the time. Instead, there's this attitude like, "I've got to go corner the market," and there's resentment, or even fear, of competition. Why would you ever be scared of competition? That's what keeps you going. That's what makes you better. That's what motivates you. At least, that's what motivates me.

I'm willing to acknowledge all the success the women before me have had, and I'm grateful for the opportunities their success has provided for me. I think of all the things I've learned from playing with and being around Teresa Edwards on the national teams and I know it's made me a stronger and better player. And when I hear Tyrone Green tell me that there's a kid who is going to be better than me on the courts in Queens these days, that makes me proud. Bring it on. Challenge me. Make me work to stay at the top.

Opening night was a whirlwind. We were home, at MCI Center, hosting the Charlotte Sting. That afternoon, I sat down and thought for a minute about what was expected of me. It's not that I was afraid I wasn't ready to play up to this new level. I believed in my game. What I feared was that I would not be able to take my entire team to a new level. I was afraid of letting down the fans, and the city, and in a way, the whole WNBA.

To be honest, though, I was more excited than nervous once I got to the arena that first night. I showed up early, because I'd already been warned that there were a lot of media outlets that wanted to talk to me before game time. I tried not to let it be a distraction. Before warm-ups and after warm-ups, I felt like I did an endless round of stand-up appearances for the local television stations. NBA Entertainment had sent a crew to follow almost my every move. There was not a single moment when I wasn't in a spotlight.

My family was coming down to the game—my mom, Davon, my grandmother, my uncle George. I didn't want to know where they were sitting, because I didn't want to get too nervous about it. Even now, it makes me nervous to have family watch me. My lawyer, Lon Babby, had promised to keep an eye out for my grandmother. And my mom and Davon planned to sit with Larry. I just concentrated on the basketball.

I remember Dawn Staley came up to me before the game to talk a little trash. "You aren't going to win," she told me. "I'm not going to let you win this game." That was all I needed to get a little extra motivation. Suddenly I was thinking about how aggressive I wanted to be from the very beginning. *She's got nothing on you,* I thought to myself. *You're bigger, you're stronger, you're even quicker than you were in college. These girls are big, but you* belong.

Anthony Williams, the mayor of D.C., tossed up the ceremonial first ball and declared the day Washington Mystics Day in the community. There was a crowd of more than twenty thousand—

though I was used to things like that after playing in so many Final Fours. Several of the Wizards sat courtside. So did Steve Francis, a University of Maryland player who had been taken with the second pick in the NBA that spring. People in the Mystics offices said he'd called and asked for tickets because he wanted to see me play.

The moment the game started, I felt myself fill with confidence. I was only out there for a second before I realized that my instincts were right: these players were a little bigger and a little stronger, but so was I. I was ready to be a pro. I belonged at this level.

It's hard to explain how that feeling develops. I missed my first shot, then made my next two. I remember making a move to the basket and, in a flash, feeling what I'd felt so often in both high school and college: *Other players can't do what you're doing. They can't keep up with your game.* I grabbed a rebound, made another shot. As the minutes went by, my confidence continued to grow.

Pretty soon the basketball just felt the same. Maybe the game was a little faster, but my place in it was exactly what it had always been. Sometimes the other team would double-down on me, and push me, and really get physical. Sometimes I'd feel like I could elevate over the entire field. The only thing different was my situation. The Mystics were not Tennessee. We weren't a team that was going to dominate at this level the way I had with the Lady Vols.

We lost that night, 83–73. I scored 18 points and had 6 rebounds. Some people tried to categorize the game as a triumph for me, if not for the franchise. I didn't like that at all. Winning is all that matters to me, not how I play or how many points I put on the scoreboard. I hated losing that night, just as much as I had hated losing every single game we lost at Tennessee.

Afterward, my life was as crazy as ever. I had to do a press conference, and there were all kinds of television cameras and reporters asking me how I felt and what I thought about the fans and the loss and my own performance and everything. Back in the locker room, my teammates were getting dressed and I was still out there, taking questions. It was almost surreal.

For some reason, my grandmother's tickets hadn't been left for her under the right name, and she'd missed the start of the game, then found herself sitting up in the nosebleed section. It took until halftime for someone to realize who she was and move her down to sit next to Lon near courtside. The cameras mobbed her too, as always, and two different networks asked her to wear a microphone so they could catch her reaction while I played. As always, my grandmother was nice, and she let them.

I tried hard to spend some time with my family after the game ended, because I knew most of them were headed back to New York that same night. My grandmother came down by the locker room, and I had to take a microphone off her and ask the NBA Entertainment crew to disappear just to be allowed a few quiet moments with her. I barely got to see Davon—I snuck out to the stands, still all sweaty in my uniform—and gave him a quick hug, and Larry ended up waiting for me forever. My pro career had begun.

Sometimes I think it surprises even me how fiercely competitive I am. Nothing's just a game. I always want to win, even when it's something silly like a relay race for a bunch of kids at a recreation center.

My nerves were wearing a little bit thin when I showed up at Fort Davis Recreation Center in southeast Washington for yet another public appearance early in my first season with the Mystics. I was late because practice went long, then Coach Darsch made us lift weights, and it's not like I can just say I have somewhere else I'm supposed to be. So by the time we got in the car to drive up to southeast, it was rush hour and we got stuck on Pennsylvania Avenue. I hate getting caught in traffic, and I knew there were all these kids waiting for me, so I started getting a little stressed.

When we got there, though, the kids didn't seem to mind one bit that I hadn't arrived on schedule. The adults didn't even seem to mind. Mostly, there were little girls there—some not even as tall as one of my legs—and they were organized in different groups, working on sliding drills and shooting drills and stuff like that. They squealed when I came in. I still can't get used to that, the way people sometimes greet me like I'm a rock star or something.

I was supposed to be guarding this girl—maybe she was fifteen—and I couldn't help myself, I was dragging her back by the arm, cheating, making sure she knew who was boss. It was fun. Even after all of it—the practice, the weights, the traffic, my being so tired—it was fun. I really do love it when I get to have events with kids.

We had a relay race after that, splitting the kids up in teams. I had a serious huddle with my team before it started.

"My line's going to win, understand?" I told them, then I turned to the girls in the line next to me and teased them. "You're going to lose!" I hooted. They just looked at me and giggled. I'm not sure if they realized I was at least half serious.

The officials said my team lost the race, but I didn't believe it. Even when the kids on the "winning team" lined up and I was giving them tickets to a Mystics game, I kept insisting that they'd cheated. I was teasing, of course. Teasing with a little truth inside. I don't lose, after all. And when I do lose, well, I admit I don't lose well.

We lost our second game in Houston on national television. That was humbling, even though I knew that the Comets were the two-time WNBA champions. I had hope for us after our preseason win in Tennessee, but this time it just didn't happen.

Our third game was in New York against the Liberty. There was a lot made of the fact that I would be playing at home and Coach Darsch would be playing against the team she coached for two seasons. I was already feeling like we were at the bottom of the league—it's hard not to think that when you haven't recorded your first victory—and I couldn't tolerate the thought of going down 0–3 in my own town.

Coach Summitt was there to do commentary for the ESPN broadcast, and we talked a little after shoot-around that morning at Madison Square Garden. As always, she had good advice for me. She said she had been watching my games so far and she didn't think that I was attacking the basket with authority the way she knew I could. As soon as she said it, I knew she was right. Sometimes, when you're playing, you focus on certain things in your game and you forget about the little things and how much of a difference they can make. I realized that I should go to the basket more, that I could draw a lot more fouls and have more of an impact. I swear, if Coach Summitt ever asked, I'd give her half of my professional paychecks. She deserves them after all she's taught me.

A lot of people came to see me play at the Garden that night, though I tried not to pay too much attention. I had friends there, and my family, and people from the neighborhood, and people who just wanted to support me because I was a hometown product. I kept hearing people yell, "Hey, what's up, Mique?" or, "Hi, Mique!" Coach Summitt noticed right away that there was a girl in the second row wearing an orange Tennessee jersey with my name on the back. I was getting used to that, but seeing it at the Garden was sweet. I was nervous and excited during warm-ups. The last time I'd been at the Garden we'd stunk it up, and I wanted to erase that memory. And the Liberty was a great defensive team, so I thought that was going to give us trouble. I never expected the game to turn out the way it did. I listened to what Coach Summitt had said that morning, and I scored 20 points. We beat New York by 22. It was their first loss of the season, and on their home court. It felt great. Afterward, they played "Native New Yorker" by Odyssey over the sound system, and I went over to Coach Summitt and gave her a big hug.

By that point, though, I'd already realized that there was not going to be anyone in the Mystics organization who would drive me and push me the way Coach Summitt had at Tennessee. I had to do it for myself. That's not something I was used to. To top it off, I was a rookie dealing with the fact that I was living in a new city—and living on my own—for the first time. I had to structure my own *life*, never mind the basketball. My grandmother wasn't there to do it for me. I didn't have Christ the King and its demanding academic and athletic schedule to help me focus. I didn't have Coach Summitt and Mickie driving me on and off the court.

I missed it most, though, on the basketball court. I know I've said it a million times, but I need structure in order to perform my best. If I do something wrong, I want someone to tell me, even if it means yelling at me the way Coach Summitt did sometimes. I need to have standards set. I need to know what's expected of me. I could care less if my coaches like me. I just wanted them to push me.

That wasn't happening in Washington. I had high hopes after the win over the Liberty, because it's hard not to get excited after a game like that. But things started to slide quickly. We lost again, and again, and with only two games to play before the All-Star break, we were 3–9. For some, that might have been viewed as an accomplishment—after all, the Mystics won just three games their entire first season. For me it was an embarrassment. Thankfully, we won our next two and then Nikki and I both were named starters on the East team for the first-ever WNBA All-Star Game. Still, I had to wonder. What good were two All-Stars if the team couldn't come together and perform? What good were we if we were halfway through the season and neither of us had figured out how we meshed together or who was going to lead this team?

Nikki was in a tough situation. I recognized that. Her first season, she had to take every shot at crunch time. Now here she is having to say, "I have another top player on my team. How does this work?" A team can certainly have more than one marquee player. It should be a blessing, not a problem. Nikki and I have two different games. We should use that to our advantage. Say Nikki's going to score 25 points a game and we're winning. That's fine by me. I'll crash the boards, I'll get the rebounds. But we have to recognize that we have two different games, and two different personalities, and figure out how to make that work. We were definitely still struggling with that then—in fact we struggled with it all season—and the coaching staff never told either of us what role they expected us to play. They were too busy trying to keep everyone happy instead.

The All-Star Game was played in New York, at Madison Square Garden, and there was a lot of hype around my playing at home again. It was really busy that weekend, and really hectic. I had so many public appearances—including a camp the league had for kids—that I think we arrived at the Garden maybe only an hour and a half before the game. I barely had time to shower and warm up.

It was fun, at first, seeing all the stars that had turned out to support women's basketball. Queen Latifah was there, and Liza Minnelli, and Whitney Houston sang the national anthem. I thought that was cool. But for me the day turned out to be a disaster. Early in the game I jammed my finger on a pass from Teresa Weatherspoon. I tried to pretend it didn't hurt and kept playing through the half. But at halftime I couldn't pretend I wasn't in pain, and it was really swelling up. New York had a hand specialist there, luckily, and they took X rays. As it turned out, I'd broken a bone in my index finger. The doctor was saying I'd be out four to six weeks, and all I could think was, *Oh my God, that's so long.* That's a big part of the season. But I've always had faith in my ability to heal. After all, hadn't I come back from a sprained MCL in less than two weeks in my sophomore season? I figured I'd only be out a few days. After all, it was my left hand, not my shooting hand. I'd figure out a way to make do.

I woke up the next day in so much pain that I had to take four painkillers to make my finger feel even close to human. It was swollen too, but I was determined to start my rehabilitation. I didn't want to miss more than a game or two. We played Detroit at MCI Center that night without me, and I was shooting to return two nights later, when we traveled to Charlotte to play the Sting. I kept remembering what Coach Summitt had said to me sophomore year about not being a baby. The first time I got injured in the WNBA, I wasn't going to let people down. They were paying me to play, and that was what I was going to do.

I played twenty-four minutes in Charlotte, and scored 9 points, but we lost again. In retrospect, I probably shouldn't have played, because my finger was killing me that night. I could barely catch the ball. The next morning it was sorer than ever. I felt like the team depended on me, though, and with our record, I didn't feel like I could miss any more minutes than I already had. Not that my presence seemed to make that much difference. We lost four straight games after the All-Star break, the fourth an ugly loss to Cleveland, a team that hadn't won a single road game all season. The Rockers didn't even have one of their starters, Suzie

McConnell Serio, and they still beat us by double digits. That's how terribly we played.

By that point, though, things had been bad for us for a long time. At least I thought so. Even before the All-Star break, we'd lost this game to Sacramento at home where we blew a lead in the second half. We just gave it away. And it wasn't the first time. The fact was, we just weren't getting it done.

After games like that, I'd drive myself crazy. I'd get pretty upset, sitting there, asking myself about a hundred questions: *Is it because we're too young? Because we're not working hard enough?* You wonder if it's ever going to get any better. On those nights, I'd go home and sit in my house, unable to sleep, and play the game over and over in my head. Sometimes, if I had a videotape, I'd watch it and try to see what we did wrong.

Pretty soon you get tired of hearing people say, "We're going to get it done tonight." You just want it to happen. We had people on that team who weren't used to losing—I was one of them—and we all got pretty frustrated, but we always knew we were in this together. We never stopped feeling like we were a team.

At times, though, it seemed to me that there wasn't enough emotion on our team. People never got too upset, and no one ever got too pumped up. It was a strange situation for me. I was used to being in locker rooms where players left every last ounce of emotion they had on the court and walked back in afterward totally drained. We almost never played like that.

My frustration just grew and grew, and it got to the point where I wasn't sure how to handle the losing anymore. This was something totally new to me, something I'd never experienced. I'd never had a losing record before, never played for a team that wasn't one of the best in its own league. Here I was, a member of one of the worst teams in the WNBA. It stung. I was so upset after every game.

Rita knew what I was going through—after all, she was used to winning at UConn and she'd had to suffer through that awful first year the Mystics had, the year before I came, when they won only three games. Rita had my total trust too. To be thrown together in a bad situation like that builds an immediate bond, and I felt like I could be totally up-front with her about how I felt. I needed somebody to open up to, and she was that person. I knew, too, that she'd never tell anyone else how I really was feeling about the season, and the coaching staff, and our team.

Rita kept telling me that we just had to keep playing, and she always told me not to blame myself for the fact that we were losing. "Mique," she'd say, "just because you're the 'star' on our team, don't blame yourself because we're not succeeding. We all have to come together and help you. You just have to keep playing the way you're capable of playing."

But it wasn't just the basketball that was bothering me, although that was definitely the main thing. Some days I felt like I called Rita and just complained and complained and complained. She was good, though. Rita never let me get away with anything. If I just started rambling—acting all self-involved—she'd pretend to fall asleep, or make some smart remark to remind me that the world does not actually revolve around me and my problems. Sometimes, she'd just tell me, "Mique, this is BS. Get over it." I needed that. I'd be acting like a drama queen or something, talking about all the millions of things in my life that were stressing me out. She kept me grounded that way.

I could talk to Rita about anything: the team, my frustrations, how exhausted I was by all the demands on my time. I could even talk to Rita about the trouble I was having with Larry. Sometimes it seemed like I was caught up in so much, but Rita was always there to listen.

RITA WILLIAMS ON CHAMIQUE

Chamique had a hard time her rookie year, and sometimes I used to think she was going to blow up my head with all the talking she did to me about her problems. I was totally cool with it, though. I knew she had a lot of stuff on her. She was going through things in her relationship with Larry. She had all these expectations coming out of college, coming to a new team. It was easy to get caught up in all of that. I think she handled it well considering that so much was surrounding her. That's hard, being a rookie and getting thrown into all of that, but I think being from Tennessee—with all the expectations and the pressure and the attention she had there—helped her a lot.

She had a hard time inside the team too, what with her and Coach Darsch not being on the same page. We had a strange situation. Chamique was the quote-unquote star on our team, but so was Nikki McCray. Nikki was our go-to person the first year, obviously. Then Chamique comes in with all these high expectations from the coaches, the fans, herself. A lot of people on the team looked up to that and knew Chamique would be a big factor on offense and defense and almost immediately considered her a leader. But personally, I don't think I ever knew who our go-to person was on that team. It was Chamique, and then it was Nikki, and it kept changing because that's the way the coaches wanted it. I think that drove Chamique a little nuts.

Chamique is the kind of person who doesn't like to step on people's toes, and that's why she handled things the way she did, I think. I'm not sure she'd ever do it again. I don't expect she will. She's too aggressive, at least on the basketball court. Off the court, she's pretty laid-back. She's like a homebody. When we would hang out, she'd usually want to watch movies, stay home. She even cooked for a few of her teammates sometimes. She's actually a good cook. Or so she says. But she'd always cook pasta, and who can't cook pasta? But don't say that to Chamique. She believes she can do everything.

Chapter 12

*A Nike-sponsored wall mural of Chamique on the outside of the MCI
Building, the Washington Mystic's home stadium. It's the building's
first mural of an athlete, and the city's largest image of a woman, ever.*

Larry came to stay with me temporarily when I first moved to
D.C. I didn't really know anyone there, and I had so much to
take care of, so I asked him to come and stay for a little while. I
needed someone to help me get adjusted, do stuff around the
house. I had training camp, two-a-days, and it's amazing how
much work it takes to get settled someplace new. And I had no
time. So I asked if he would help me, if he would take care of a lot
of the little things. He said yes.

Our big misunderstanding was about his coming to stay with
me. He thought I was asking him to move in, and I really just
wanted him to stay for a little while, until I was settled. I couldn't
live with a guy—my grandmother would kill me! But when I finally
asked him to leave, he got really upset.

By then, though, things had changed. We had changed. I was a
different person than I was when we first started dating at Tennessee, and so was he. I had so much going on in my life, and I
wasn't ready to be in that serious a relationship. And he could
sense things were different too, and he wasn't happy about it.

My grandmother wasn't pleased about him being in D.C. anyway. She kept telling me, "Chamique, this is your time. Everything

you worked hard for is yours now, and you need to enjoy your life, enjoy everything that's coming to you, and not get too caught up in other things." She told me I needed to experience life. I could see what she was saying. I'd never really dated all that much before Larry. And I didn't like the way I felt—like I had to report back to him all the time.

Things became pretty clear to me one night when I was out with my teammates and some friends and I was excited and having a great time. We stayed out really late, and when I got back, he was upset and questioning me about where I'd been all day, what I'd been doing, and that's when it hit me. *I'm not ready for this. I'm not ready to have someone question how I spend my time.* So we broke up.

I'm over it now, of course, but it makes you think a lot. You expect a person like that to be in your life forever, but it doesn't always work out that way. It doesn't work out that way most of the time, I guess. At first I kept thinking, *I've been with this person for two and a half years, and I think I know him and I think he knows me, and now—waaa!—it's over.* For a while, I couldn't believe it. But it just didn't work. It wasn't his fault, it wasn't my fault. It just didn't work.

My breakup only compounded what was a real up-and-down summer. For a pretty good stretch, our team seemed lost. We didn't play like a unit. We had so little chemistry. By August 1, we were 8–17, had lost eight of our last nine games, and were tied for last in the league with Cleveland. I got even more introverted then. I was always asking myself, *What's the problem? What are we doing wrong?* I stayed to myself, because I was so frustrated. Rita said she could always tell when I was down because I'd be so quiet and keep to myself. Usually, in the locker room I'd be joking with her and Nikki and Monica Maxwell, but during that stretch I didn't do that much. And I don't know if that was a bad thing or a good thing to do at the time. I just felt like I didn't want to bring my teammates down, or dump all the frustration I was feeling on them. Rita was the only one I really let go with. She was the one who was there when I needed to vent.

When I wasn't at practice or games, I still tried to leave it behind.

I'd hang out with my friends, go shopping. I'd hang with Rita too, though she'd never go shopping with me. She hated the way I shopped. I like to look at a lot of things when I'm in a store. I'm a big shopper. It drove Rita nuts. She'd say, "Mique, you go into a store and you have to look at every single shirt. You unfold it, hold it up to yourself, refold it. *Every single shirt.*" So whenever I asked her to go shopping, she'd be like, "Nope. No way. Not with you."

Mostly, though, I tried to focus all my energy on basketball. Before the season had started, I'd told Lon and Jim—my lawyers—that I wanted to knock out as many of my responsibilities as I possibly could. The commercials, the photo shoots, all those things that came with my endorsement contracts—I wanted to do all that beforehand, so I could really concentrate once I was playing. I still had to do some things. When we were in Los Angeles on a road trip, I filmed my first Nike commercial. It was a long day, but it was fun.

I had told the Nike people that I wanted the commercial to have a personal touch, and they came up with a couple of different options. I chose the one where I recite parts of Psalm 23, because it meant something special to me, and I liked that. I didn't know, though, how people were going to perceive it. I didn't know if they'd say, "Oh, they're trying to use religion to market sports," and see that as a bad thing. In the end, it got positive and negative feedback. There were religious groups who said it was the first time a high-profile athlete promoted both faith and athletics in a commercial—though there are certainly a lot of athletes that talk about their faith all the time. I just wanted the commercial to show something about who I am as a person, not just a basketball player, and I thought it did. My grandmother liked it too.

Once the team was really struggling, though, I told Lon and Jim that I didn't want to do anything outside basketball that wasn't absolutely necessary. We had to turn things around. And we did. For almost two weeks, we went on a winning streak. Our defensive intensity picked up incredibly. Coach Darsch was getting into it, and she really gave us this energy. We won three games in a row, then four, then a magic number five against the Liberty at MCI Center. That one we won in overtime. I remember I stopped

Teresa Weatherspoon on the way to the basket in the closing seconds of the game.

During the streak, I played some of the best basketball I'd played in my career, and I wasn't measuring myself by the number of points I put on the board. I was playing defense, great defense, and my teammates had started to follow me. I was so excited, after so many weeks of frustration, and I was doing everything I could to get the team pumped up. And people were finally responding. We had emotion those two weeks. I remember Valerie Still standing on the sidelines screaming at me, "They're in lockdown. You've got them shut down. This is your team!" It was exhilarating.

Valerie's arrival in Washington—the Mystics signed her on June 30—made a huge difference to me. Until then, I'd had my friendship with Rita and a pretty good relationship with most of my team, but I didn't feel like I had leadership. I didn't have anyone there to teach me and help me figure out my role in this franchise. Valerie is thirty-eight years old, and she was an all-star when she played for the Columbus Quest in the ABL. She has a lot of experience. So when Val came to Washington, she not only supported me but started to hold me accountable for what I was doing on the court, almost like a coach. That's what I'd been missing all season. That's what Coach Summitt always did. That's what I need.

When the Meeks arrived at Tennessee, Coach Summitt told me that it was my job to turn us all into a team and be the driving force. When I came to Washington, the Mystics coaches told me they didn't want to put too much pressure on me and I thought that was not really productive. I was getting paid what I was getting paid because I was expected to be a top player. I had a job to do. I wanted to scream at the coaching staff, "Don't limit me because you don't want to overwhelm me with something. Challenge me. *Challenge me.*" They never once told me I *had* to do something, that I was responsible for picking the team up or making the key shot. Well, somebody needs to be responsible. And I know the coaches were trying to protect me, but I *wanted* that responsibility.

It was toward the middle of the season when Melissa McFerrin, our assistant coach, came to me and said, "You have to lead this team, and follow behind no one. We know you can score, and we know you can get us ten rebounds a game." That's when I finally kicked it into gear and started playing really hard on defense. And inside, I was kicking myself. *C'mon, Mique!* I told myself. *It took you this long to figure this out!*

On August 14, we beat the Los Angeles Sparks, for our sixth straight victory. We moved within half a game of the third and final Eastern Conference play-off spot, in a battle with Detroit and Orlando. I felt like we controlled our own destiny. We were play-ing the Orlando Miracle at home the following night. A win would put us in control. And that's what we were all feeding off: one game to get into the play-offs. We wanted to surprise people, to show them that the Mystics could make the postseason.

Then I had my heart broken all over again. I just remember Orlando playing with so much fire that night. We came out so flat. I was standing out there, and I felt like we just didn't know what to do. After we lost, and all our play-off hopes were dead, I just kept thinking: *Never again. Never again do I want to feel like this. This can-not happen next year. This is what I do. This is my job. I can't be feeling like this. Never do I want to be labeled a loser.* And there we were, losing and losing and losing. People would say, "She's good, but they're a losing team." I don't want that. Never again.

Things finally blew up between Coach Darsch and me the final game of the season. I don't usually get like that—blow up on the court, in the game—but I did this time. I think it was because everything from the whole season had built up in me, and it all came out at once.

Coach Darsch and I had what I'll call a conflict of interest. I didn't feel like we were attacking the situation the way we should have, and I was like: *This has been the situation all season long. It's wrong.* I was upset and she was upset, and she said something to me during the game and I just blew up. I looked at her, and then I walked to my seat on the bench, saying, "This is the same damn thing that's been going on all season." I think she didn't like my attitude then. So she benched me.

I remember one of the players on my team saying, "Mique, handle it with class." That's exactly what I did. The people in the stands probably couldn't figure out why I wasn't playing anymore. I stayed on the bench, cheering on my team for the rest of the game. I didn't show what I was feeling. But inside, I was frustrated by how things had played out and how the coaching staff hadn't taken a lot of initiative to correct that. And I tell you: I won't ever let myself be in that situation again.

You have to understand, I love the fans in Washington. I love the city, I love my team. But I'm supercompetitive, and I couldn't tolerate the situation we had my first season. It was all about making excuses. Excuses, excuses, and more excuses. It made me sick.

I'm not one to wait around for things to happen, and that first season I did way too much waiting around. I kept telling myself, *It's going to get better!* But it didn't. I always believed what Coach Summitt taught me: When you struggle, that's when you realize what you're made of, and that's when you realize what the people around you can do. You learn who you'd want to take with you to a war, and who you'd only want to take to lunch.

Still, I didn't get down on Coach Darsch a single time while we still were fighting for a play-off spot because I know you need to respect your coaches. I kept everything I was feeling to myself for the entire year. I thought that was the best way to handle things. If things were going to work at all in my second season, though, I felt it was necessary to clear the air. I just felt we needed to communicate.

I had a meeting with Melissa—she was still our assistant coach then, though she later got promoted to general manager—two months before training camp and my second pro season. I admit I really got on her, almost made her cry. Most of the time, I'm too hesitant to speak my mind in these situations. I'm too nice, and people try to take advantage of that. I wasn't willing to do that anymore. This is my job. My profession. My reputation. I can't work for anyone who tolerates excuses. It would drive me crazy. If I'm going to be nice, I'm going to sit back and just try to fit in. Well, if you want to be successful in life, you can't just fit in. You have to be who you are and learn how to excel as that person. For an entire season I sacrificed myself to be within the team as our coaching staff defined it, and we were horrible. Horrible. I'm not willing to let that happen again.

The Wizards' general manager, Wes Unseld, kept telling me, "Shoot more! Shoot more!" and my response to that was, "Right! I need to be more aggressive." Even the fans who sat near courtside were yelling the same thing. "Shoot more! Shoot more!" I know I can score, and I can get my shot off when we need it. But I believed that wasn't what my coaching staff wanted from me, and we never took the time to sit down and figure out how to best use me in different situations. Coach Darsch is a good coach when it comes to Xs and Os, and she's a great defensive coach, but it takes time to get to know her, so we never really communicated. And it took me the whole season to realize that, in that way, Coach Darsch is a lot like me. It was only after the season was over that I realized that was our problem. How can you communicate when you have *two* people who have walls up? In the off-season, though, we've worked really hard to get to know each other. We went from being two people who never said much more than hi and good-bye to calling each other on the phone to see how things were going. It's a huge change in our relationship.

I have to realize too, that not everyone is going to be Coach Summitt, and I can't make her the standard against which I measure all my other coaches. She's tough, and as a player and a person, I seem to need that. I'd love to play for her again. She's not trying to be my friend, she's trying to make me win. And that's the thing with me—I don't need my coach to be my friend. I don't even need my teammates to be my friends. What I need is respect—both ways. I need to respect my coach, and I need my coach to respect me. The same goes for the team. We don't have to like one another to play well together, we just have to respect one another's abilities and work hard and we will accomplish what we've set out to accomplish. We just need to have the same passion for the game and for reaching our goals.

That summer with the Mystics, we had this crazy idea that keeping everyone in the locker room happy was the best way to win basketball games. "Don't hurt anyone's feelings" was like our motto. I'm not talking about the way we treated one another as human beings. Of course, I believe that we all should treat one another well. I'm talking about the way decisions were made on the basketball court. We'd actually run systems that were designed to give everyone a chance, as if we were playing ball in some seventh-grade physical education class, where giving each girl a chance to discover her own talents is the objective. As professionals, we should have had only one objective: to win. That's what should have driven our decision-making process, and in my opinion, it never did.

At times it got ridiculous. I think by the end of the season everyone on the team knew that I was the go-to player in clutch situations, but it was never said out loud because no one wanted a confrontation. We're not kids. We're professionals. Acting like that is not what the women's game needs.

We don't need to get along to win basketball games. This is our job. What we need to do is all be responsible, and want to win, and have the same goal. I take my job very seriously. I know I need to play better than I did my first season. I know I need to step up more, but I also need to know that everyone will be held accountable, superstar or not. We lose as a team, we win as a team.

Things have to change our second season. If we don't make the play-offs in August, I'm going to come home after the Olympics in September and go on vacation for a month. It will take at least that long for me to recover if I have to suffer that kind of devastation again. I understand that we're the youngest team in the league and one day we could really be something special. And I so much want to be a part of that—when it happens, if it happens. But we have to become more mature in our approach this year. We have to attack situations differently. That includes me, I have work to do too, but I don't feel that I can keep playing under the circumstances I had to play under my first season. It was just too frustrating for me.

All during that first season, I kept flashing back to things Coach Summitt had said to me. I remember in a game against Vanderbilt, I was struggling at halftime, and she screamed at me, "You're supposed to be the best player in the country? Holdsclaw, you only have five points and three rebounds! Are you going to prove yourself, or what?"

In my first Washington season, no one ever held me accountable. Maybe I needed to hold myself accountable. I accept that. I understand that I need to be self-motivated. Self-motivation should carry you at least 85 percent of the way. But that other 15 percent is pushed out of you by other people—your coaches, your teammates, the opposition. The 1999 season, I felt like I needed to be 99 percent self-motivated, and that's a hard level to keep up by yourself. I also need to feel like I trust and believe in the people around me. One of the reasons I used to get so mad at my mother was because she'd make promises and never follow through on them. She'd say she was committed to something, but she never really was. To do that to me now, it's like burning a bridge. Because of who I am, I have a difficult time accepting it, and a difficult time forgiving. I need people to keep their word. When someone gives me their word, I consider it a bond. You don't break that. Ever.

With all of these pressures and frustrations in my life now, my need for friends to talk to and relax with are just as great as—and sometimes even greater than—it was when I was in college. But I have to admit, it's harder to find new people whom I can totally relax with now that my life has changed so much. Everything I worried about when I first went to college—why does this person want to be friends with me? can I trust this person?—is only intensified now that I'm a pro. I don't want to sound like I'm naturally distrustful of people, but I think I have to be careful. Even my grandmother tells me that.

One of the new friends I made was Steve Francis. Having him in my life really helped me my first year in Washington, because he was able to understand my life in a way that few people can, and I could do the same for him. Everything I was going through my first year as a pro, he was about to go through in the NBA in his rookie season, which started that fall.

It's funny, sometimes, how these things happen. I'd met him a few years before I moved to D.C., at a Final Four when I was in college. He'd asked to get introduced then, which I thought was kind of nice. We got reintroduced right after I arrived in Washington by a woman who works for the Mystics. As it turns out, she was Steve's baby-sitter when he was little and has known him for a long time. She told me one day that Steve wanted to meet me—we never really talked that one time in college, we were both too shy—and I said fine, so she set it up.

We hit it off right off the bat, and started spending a lot of time together by August. It was easy for us to hang out, because we liked a lot of the same things. It's funny, we actually had the same car— the exact same car. Mine had a gold kit, his had a silver kit, but they were almost twins. Because he was from the area and had played at Maryland, he took me around town a lot at the end of that summer and would show me different places. We went to Dave & Buster's to play arcades. We went to the movies. He showed me here, took me there. His training camp for the Houston Rockets hadn't started yet, so he was around a lot.

Mostly, though, our bond came through how much we had in common in our lives and our careers. We talked so much. I could complain to him about how badly things were going with the Mystics, and he'd always tease me, say, "Man! Your team sucks!" And then once his season started and he had a rough game or they lost, he could call me and just say, "Aaaaah, man!" and I'd totally understand. I was like, "Been there, done that." I felt like we were two people taking similar paths in different worlds. We both even ended up in the same situation—both of us won rookie of the year awards, and both of us missed the play-offs. It helped a lot having someone who understood—exactly—what that was like.

But I tell you, I'd give my award back in a second if it meant our season would have ended differently.

TERESA EDWARDS ON CHAMIQUE

The first time Chamique was on the national team, she was just a happy-go-lucky kid who didn't know what to expect. I think she thought it was supposed to be a summer vacation, but she soon learned it was going to be a lot of work. She was just a kid then, but I think she's done a lot of growing up mentally because she's been through so many different challenges, on and off the court. She's faced with the stardom thing, and she's had to grow up fast. There's a lot of responsibility that comes with every dollar you make, and I think Chamique understands that.

The Olympics are probably going to be the most valuable experience of her life and the most valuable challenge to her growth in the game. Not being among the best players would show that she was afraid of challenging herself to be the best she truly can be. But Chamique has shown that she's willing to do that and willing to sacrifice and learn her role with the other players. It's going to be really valuable in terms of advancing her career.

I think Chamique's great now, but she can be even better. After the national team tour, she can become more of an asset and play a bigger role. But it's up to Chamique to realize that. I don't think she understands that she can make that decision, rather than wait for a coach to define her role.

That's one thing about Chamique: she's got to learn to do it herself. Sometimes she seems like she's playing on autopilot and she's still getting it done, at least as far as what you see on the stat sheets. But Chamique hasn't come close to realizing what she can really do. That's what I believe. And I will probably always be that one person who challenges her. I see more in her. I see a totally dominant player. She just has to make it happen.

Chapter 13

The U.S. national team in September 1999.

After my last Mystics game that first year, I was really in need of a break, so I took Davon and Rita down to Tennessee for a week to hang out with my friends and coaches. When I'm stressed and down it always helps to talk to Coach Summitt. That's a big change from our relationship when I was a freshman, but it's true—we've come a long way. Mostly, though, this time what I needed to do was just relax and have a good time. I needed a vacation.

When I left Tennessee, I went to New York to see my friends and my grandmother. My body was so tired, but that wasn't what worried me most. I was really mentally fatigued. I'd been playing basketball for three years without a break, and it had taken a toll on me. I was supposed to join the U.S. national team in San Diego in a few weeks to start preparing for the first of our pre-Olympic tours, and I didn't know if I had what it was going to take. There wasn't enough time for me to get over my exhaustion, not to mention my disappointment and frustration over how the season had ended.

When I got to San Diego, I was still completely drained mentally and I started to think that I didn't want to be there at all. It's a passion of mine to be an Olympian—I didn't want to throw that away—but all I kept thinking was, *I don't know if I can do this.* Our schedule was difficult. Not only did we have practices—sometimes two a day—but we also traveled a lot. We had a tour in the United States, where we played against women's college teams, and we also went to Italy, Eastern Europe, and Brazil to play exhibitions. Those are great places, but it only adds to your exhaustion to be getting on so many planes. And the schedule was going to take us almost all the way up to the start of the next WNBA season, and then we'd all have to go straight from the season to a minicamp before heading to Sydney. It seemed like forever to me.

It wasn't long before I started to hint to people that I might just walk away. I called Coach Summitt. I called Mickie. I called my lawyers and asked them what I could do. I don't know how to explain it, except to say that when you're that mentally tired, you start to think crazy. So there I was, thinking about giving up the chance to represent my country at the Olympics in Sydney. It certainly sounds crazy now. Nell Fortner, the Olympic coach, sat me down at one point and tried to be reassuring. She told me that it may seem like a long time, but it wasn't really. Coach Summitt wrote me a letter then too, telling me to hang in there. She's the one who pointed out to me that when you get mentally tired, you make crazy decisions. She reminded me again that tough times don't last, but tough people do. And I believe that.

Still, though, I was shot. I just didn't believe I could do it. I was just so tired. So very, very tired. People kept reminding me what a great opportunity this was for me. They all were right, but for a while I couldn't see it. Eventually, though, I came out of it. I tried to think about how many people would want a chance like this. I heard what Coach Summitt said about how toughing it out would make me stronger. I decided to stay.

I made it through our first camp, and a trip to Palo Alto to play in a tournament, which we won. After that, they gave us almost a three-week break. I went to visit Steve in Houston for a few days, and to visit another friend, and then I went home to New York for nine days and just rested and spent time with my family. My house may be in Washington, but home for me is still my grandmother's apartment. It's where I will always go to relax.

Having had that break made it a lot easier to return to training. When I came back, in November, it was with renewed energy—so it was frustrating when, shortly after that, I pulled my groin muscle and had to miss two and a half weeks of training. I couldn't wait to recover from my injury and get back on the court.

I'm the youngest player on the Olympic team. At twenty-two (I'll turn twenty-three before the Olympics start) I'm very conscious of the fact that I'm the baby. A lot of the other players are the great women players who dominated in the Atlanta Olympics four years ago. Teresa Edwards is back again, along with Lisa Leslie, Dawn Staley, my teammate Nikki McCray from the Mystics, all those guys. Being the youngest does make a difference, but it's not as big a deal as it was that summer I first played with the U.S.A. team—that summer after my sophomore year of college. The other players still look out for me now, like I'm their little sister or something, but everyone treats me cool. I've been around all those guys for so long at this point that I'm used to them and they are used to me.

Teresa, especially, is someone I've really gotten to know well. She's a friend, but she's also somebody I respect and look up to, someone who just challenges me. She's seen everything and been through a lot, and I try to take from her whatever I can that will help better me and take my game to another level. It's not at all insulting to me to be given orders or directions from someone like Teresa. She does it all the time—and I listen. I know I'm young and don't know everything. I appreciate it. I'll be on the court, passing the ball, and Teresa will say, "C'mon, Mique! You've got to be strong with it!" She'll yell at me to move on defense. She likes to tell people that the U.S.A. team is the only place where I can be a kid, spread my wings.

It's true. I learn a lot from being on that team. Yes, I'm a good player, but this is a place where I have a chance to grow and make mistakes without feeling like I'm responsible for carrying the whole team, the way I did in Tennessee or the way I did a lot of the time when the Mystics were struggling my first season. With the Olympic team, I feel like I can work on so many things, and that's truly a blessing. I'm grateful for this experience. Often, in my life, I feel like a kid growing into an adult world, but at times my situation with the Olympic team reminds me of the first years I lived with my grandmother and the things she said to me then. She wanted me to enjoy being a kid. In a way, that's what I'm doing on this team. At times, I'll do something goofy and it will just be . . . okay.

The whole situation almost seems unreal sometimes. Of course, the Olympics *are* real, but they only happen every four years and you learn special things. You're in a special situation. I have to be realistic: never again will I be on a team with that much talent—at least, not unless I'm on another Olympic team. It's not an everyday situation. So sometimes there's almost this feeling that we're invincible.

It also creates different situations for all of us, playing on a team like this. You have a whole bunch of players who are used to being the go-to player on their own teams, but we can't all be that here. My role on this team is different than it will be on any other team I ever play on, but I have to accept that. That's the only way we can take our game to another level as a team. The media's always comparing us to the men's dream team with Michael Jordan that won the gold medal at the Olympics in Barcelona in 1992. And if you think about that team, Michael Jordan wasn't even the leading scorer. That's how it works in this situation, where you just have to go out and play your role to the best of your ability. Nobody is the real leader. On any given night, somebody different steps up. There have been games when I've had double-doubles, games when Nikki steps up . . . everybody has a night.

What the coaches want from me, I think, is to just come in and bring energy and athleticism. They want me to play hard and contribute. I've always played small forward, but on this team I'm a big guard. In international play, guards are big, and we need that. I'm steadily improving in that role. I'm a rebounder. I can create off the dribble. I'm just out there learning.

I don't remember much about past Olympics—my only real Olympic hero was Jackie Joyner-Kersee, who is really the athlete I looked up to most as a kid. I admit, I didn't even watch the women's basketball team win the gold medal in Atlanta in 1996. I know, though, how much people expect out of us in Sydney. I don't consider it pressure, but we know that people expect a lot. There are doubters already too. People say we've overtrained and we're going to be burned out, and other people are worried about team chemistry since we've had to split up for the WNBA season and will only get back together to train briefly before going to Australia. I consider those doubts to be motivation. We sacrificed the whole off-season to this, and there's no way we're going to go out there and lose. We built a bank account during all that time we spent together, and that's what we're going to draw on when we get back. Our schedule is just the way it has to work here with the WNBA, and we can't change that. Sure, we'll have to get used to playing together again, but mentally, I think, we all feel like we can do whatever it is we have to do.

Despite how burned out I felt after last year's WNBA season, I don't have any worries that I'll feel exhausted again when we get to Sydney. This is crunch time, and like Coach Summitt always says, I'm at my best at crunch time. There will be a lot of time to rest after the Olympics are over, in October. I'll get my rest then. My off-time will be then. The Olympics are going to be my total focus. I'm excited about it. This is a big thing: the Olympics, on center stage. It's no time to be tired, and I believe that if you set your mind to something—and my mind is focused on winning the gold medal—the image of that success can be your motivation.

That fall after my first WNBA season, though, the Olympics seemed so far away and it was hard to focus. The injury only made it worse. It's hard when you feel like you're out of the loop, which is what happens when you get hurt and can't practice. There we were, starting up something that's really going to be incredible—we were going to the Olympics!—and I wasn't able to fully participate.

By late November, though, I was back at full strength. We were on a national tour, playing college teams across the country. (The only team we lost to was . . . Tennessee. I think Coach Summitt liked that.) Then we got to take a really long break over the holidays before meeting up back in Miami to prepare for a tour in Eastern Europe. By then, I was feeling good about everything again.

Later that winter was when I heard about the changes for my *other* team: the Mystics had lost Rita Williams in the WNBA expansion draft. The WNBA is young, but it's been growing every season—there were eight teams for the league's first season, in 1997, and there are sixteen now—and to help the new teams get off the ground, they hold an expansion draft to redistribute the players. The Mystics had to leave some players vulnerable in the draft, and Rita was one of them. It shocked me a little, because Rita was my only real friend on the team, and for a moment I worried about what I'd do without her, but honestly, I was mainly just happy for her. She's my buddy, and she didn't get the opportunities she really wanted in Washington. Of course, I'll miss her after all we went through that season, and the way she was always there for me. We were always saying that one day—one day—the Mystics would run the league. Let them laugh at us now, we said, but we're the youngest team and one day we'll show them. That's one of the ways our team stuck together so well. So I admit I was thinking about how Rita wouldn't be around for that. Instead, like she told me on the phone, she'll be trying to play her best games against the Mystics.

With all the time I spent playing and training with the Olympic team those months, I barely had a break because I had so many other responsibilities at the same time. In February, I went to San Jose to be a part of the NBA All-Star Game weekend. The Wizards didn't have an All-Star, but Richard Hamilton came to play with me in the two-ball competition. Steve was there too, playing two-ball with Cynthia Cooper from the Comets, and he was talking a lot of trash, saying they were going to kill us. Richard and I wound up finishing last, and Steve and Cynthia were bad too, so it turned out to be pretty funny.

The weekend was pretty crazy because I had a lot of public appearances, that kind of thing. The day of the two-ball competition, I had to get up at like 4:30 A.M. to get to one of the shows I had to do. Still, the whole weekend was pretty cool for me. My friend Rashard—the one who used to ride the bus with me to Christ the King—came along, and there were a lot of great parties. It was fun just being in that kind of environment. I had an opportunity to meet a lot of players, like Vince Carter, Tracy McGrady, Kobe Bryant, Shaq. What I liked the most was getting to know the younger players—like Vince and Tracy, the young generation. It's cool how down-to-earth they are. They're young like me, and cordial and easy to get along with. That's how I've always wanted people to look at me. It's part of why my closest friends are still Cheron and Anthony, and why I wanted Rashard to come to the All-Star weekend with me.

Also during that winter, I was part of a video that PBS made for Black History Month. That meant a lot to me because it meant that I got to be a voice for my community. I was also part of an ABC special on athletes for the new millennium that featured people like Tiger Woods and Derek Jeter of the Yankees. Gatorade asked me to film a commercial, and I had photo shoots in New York and Boca Raton, Florida, and another Nike commercial to shoot. That commercial was the one that had Michael Jordan in it too, though Michael wasn't there the day I filmed. His part was shot separately.

All these appearances came to a climax in the spring when I attended the Naismith Awards. This was my third year doing so—every year they give out awards for high school and college players of the year, and I'd won at both levels—but this time was extra special. Because it was 2000, they were giving out special century awards as well. Coach Summitt was named the women's college coach of the century, and I was named the women's player, and Tamika was there too, because she was women's college player of the year. For me it was a tremendous honor, one made more special by the fact that Coach Summitt and I were sharing the award. Kareem Abdul-Jabbar won men's college player of the century and John Wooden won for coach, so both the player and the coach came from the same team on that side too. I think that said something important: that no matter how great a player you are, it takes a great coach to really bring that out of you and make you successful. I know Coach Summitt did that for me.

At first, the importance of the Naismith Award went over my head a little bit. It's hard for something like that to sink in: player of the *century*. I was told that the voting had been neck-and-neck between Cheryl Miller and me, and then they started to get a ton of votes for me at the end. I thought that was so cool. Six years before, I'd been to that same ceremony in Atlanta to win the high school player of the year, and that was the first time I'd ever spoken in front of a crowd like that. It was a big moment for me. I felt like a kid when I went up there, even though I'd practiced and practiced my speech.

This time, I still felt like a kid, and maybe that's why what I said sounded a little goofy. "Gosh, player of the century and I'm only twenty-two years old!" I told the crowd. Everybody started laughing. I laughed too. Maybe a lot has happened in those six years, and maybe I've grown up a lot, but there's still that part of me that my grandmother always encouraged. The part that got excited. The part that thought, *Wow, this is great!* The part that sometimes still feels like an eleven-year-old shooting hoops in the projects, the whole future stretching out before me, the possibilities endless.

At home during this time, my mom was getting a new house that I was helping her buy, and Davon was thinking about colleges. I really wanted him to go, but I didn't talk about it to him too much, because I didn't want to put any pressure on him. I told him to take his time, figure out what he wants. He's young, and I don't want him making a decision just because it's something I want. He knows my grandmother wants him to go to school too, so I can't imagine that he won't graduate someday.

What I want him to know, though, is that even after graduating from college, even after leaving it so far behind in many ways, it continues to play a big part in my life. I continue to learn from those relationships in Tennessee and from my old team. For all my frustrations during my years there—both with Coach Summitt at first, and with the place being so small and so country—I still love to go back. I met some of the most important people in my life there, and had some of my most memorable moments.

Needless to say, then, when the NCAA Tournament came around that first spring after graduation, I followed my team pretty closely. Tamika had become the best player in the country and was getting a lot of attention, and people were wondering if Tennessee could wind up back on top again.

The Olympic team was scheduled to play an exhibition game in Philadelphia during the women's Final Four, so I was really rooting for the team to get there, because then I'd get to see Coach Summitt and Mickie and everyone else. I was so proud of them, because they'd had their losses and a pretty tough season, but they made it to the Final Four anyway, which was great. I was so psyched. Kellie decided to come up for the weekend too, and she was waiting for me in front of the hotel when our bus got there that first day. It's funny, but I hadn't seen Kellie since her wedding and we don't talk on the phone constantly like I do with some of my friends, but it only took a few minutes before I felt like we were right back where we'd left off. It's like that with Kellie. Her husband, Jon, was there too. We sat together for the semifinals, and I wore sophomore Michelle Snow's other jersey, which I got from Coach Summitt. Even though we were only on the team together for a year, Michelle is a pretty good friend of mine now. Coach Summitt says she looks up to me, and so when I heard her mother couldn't come to the Final Four because she was sick, I wanted to show her some support. I teased her before the game, told her that if I was wearing her jersey, she'd better not go out there and play like a sucker.

It was so hard to watch those guys lose so badly to UConn in the final. I kept thinking that I wanted to be out there, playing with them. I wanted to go out there and help them, but I knew I couldn't. My time was over. Still, those guys are like my little sisters. I played with them, and it hurt so much to watch. I'm not used to being a fan—it's a different feeling—and there was a passion that I felt sitting up there that I wish I could have given to them.

After the game was over, I went into the locker room, and people were sobbing and upset, and I remembered what that felt like from when I lost my senior year. What I remember most, though, was Kara Lawson—she's a freshman—taking it so hard. She was in the corner crying, and I looked at her and just said, "Get that girl a tissue." But I had so much respect for her that day. What I saw from her in that locker room showed me that she's a real competitor. She's a player with real heart, and I could understand her, because I knew I would have been that person sitting in the corner crying. I *was* that person. I wanted to tell her that that's what drives you to succeed later, feeling that kind of pain. But I'll tell you this: Kara is going to be a good one. I could see that.

Right after Final Four weekend, I had my foot X-rayed because it had been giving me a lot of trouble, and I got some bad news: I had two stress fractures. The doctors were predicting that I'd be out for about six weeks, which meant I'd miss all of Mystics training camp and maybe even part of the season, but I wasn't too worried. I've always been a fast healer and I knew I'd be back on the court during camp, even if I did have to struggle for a few weeks first with a boot on my foot. And in fact, I was right. I made it back in time to participate in training camp and start in the Mystics season opener the last day of May. We won that night, and I came away from the game feeling really good about our team and the way we showed a lot of pride on the court. Let's hope it's a sign for the whole season to come.

Chapter 14

Chamique holding her cousin Kassala, daughter of her uncle Thurman Holdsclaw—the man who first put a basketball in Chamique's hands and encouraged her to play.

My grandmother still lives in the same apartment at Astoria Houses. People ask me all the time why I haven't bought her a big house in the suburbs, or helped her get settled back home in Alabama. The truth is, I've offered, but she's just never taken me up on it.

When I first started asking, my grandmother always said things like, "When I retire, Chamique, that's when I'll go back to Alabama." And I accepted that. But as the date of her retirement got closer and closer, she never said anything more about moving. So one day that first winter after I became a pro, when I was home visiting, I pressed her on it a little. "Grandma," I said, "what do you want to do? Your retirement is coming up. I have to start making plans."

The next thing I knew, she was crying. She told me that once you get older, it's hard to leave your friends. And her friends are in Astoria. She talked about missing people in the building, about missing Miss Hayes down the block. She kept telling me that it's harder to make friends once you're older. She has her own little world, her community, at Astoria Houses. It's hard for her to let that go.

In my heart I have to admit I'm glad my grandmother feels that way. It's hard to describe what I feel when I go back to Astoria now, when I take the shuttle up to LaGuardia and catch a cab into my neighborhood, or drive myself up from D.C. I don't look at the streets or the buildings and compare them to the pristine neighborhood where I live now. I don't see my grandmother's cramped apartment and compare it to my town house in Alexandria. I just see home. To me, this is where I'm from, this is my reality. I can't be more blessed than to have seen the best of both worlds. It makes me who I am, and I'm not ashamed to say I'm proud of that.

I've tried to explain what drives me, what pushes me, and a lot of that is where I'm from. My grandmother has played a huge role in making me who I am. But on a very basic level, what pushes me is my brother—to see him grow up and to see him know that just because things are bad, that doesn't mean they won't turn around, that you can't turn them around. I think that's why I feel so blessed in my life now. That's why I care so much about my family—knowing what we've been through, and here we are today. My mother has a nice house in the suburbs, in Westchester County. My father is living in Brooklyn. Davon finished high school in June 2000. I'm so proud of him. But my grandmother still lives in Astoria. A part of me still lives there too.

Nike has promised to do over my court, the middle park, and wants to put my name on it. This was my court, after all. This is my 'hood. These are my people. I have to set an example for them. That's how I look at it. There are a lot of ignorant people here who live in ways that I wouldn't approve of, but there are also a lot of good people who just need an opportunity. I want to make sure those kids see those opportunities and realize that they can do different things.

I go home to my neighborhood now, and there are girls on the middle park playing ball. There are girls' teams at the Boys and

Girls Club. Tyrone says he has a girl there who is going to be better than me. I go to Madison Square Garden to play the New York Liberty and there are girls lined up to get my autograph, all wearing "Holdsclaw" jerseys. When I was younger and got lucky enough to go to the Garden to see a game, it was never to see women, that much is for sure.

I have little boys wearing my jersey now. How cool is that? Before, they might have been teased, "Why are you wearing a *girl's* jersey?" Now they just tell me, "You're my favorite." It's so cute.

I get letters from people who are incarcerated. I get letters from people who have lived their whole life in Queens and remember me from Christ the King. Those letters often talk about how they used to watch me play in high school, or how they don't live too far away from where I grew up. "Just to know somebody from our neighborhood could go out there and accomplish the things you've accomplished and make it makes me proud." That's what they write to me. People write that they remember the other kids making fun of me, or they remember coming home on the train and walking to their building and seeing this skinny girl on the court. And how it makes them feel good now, to know where I've ended up. I've gotten tons of letters just from little kids who have read the story about my relationship with my grandmother.

One day I was signing autographs after a Mystics game, and a little girl came up to me. She was shy, but she wanted to talk.

"You know," she said, "I have the same family situation. I read your stories over and over again. I really use it for inspiration."

You hear that, and it makes everything worthwhile. It motivates me. I couldn't care less about all the hype and stuff. It's the people who are really feeling me who touch me. People are starting to learn what I'm all about, about my personal situation, my childhood, my life. It's not easy to talk about. Especially for kids. It's so easy for kids to feel bad about themselves because of their situation. If my life makes it easier for them to talk about it themselves, makes them more comfortable, that makes me feel like I've really accomplished something.

Kids see me on TV now, and they see me driving a nice car or living in a nice house, and I worry that they think everything has always been dandy for me. That it's always been like this, and it's not something that they can have for themselves.

What I want them to know is I worked hard for this. My family struggled. I didn't grow up in the best neighborhood. I come from a broken home. But I wanted something for myself, I had a dream and aspirations. And I had one person—my grandmother—who kept me on the right path. I had one person who wanted to see me succeed and put so much into me and into making that happen.

Whatever I do now, I always think about my grandmother. When I'm tired, or I don't feel like I want to do something I should, I think about all the hard work she's put into me to make me who I am today. And when I go out there and play basketball or give a speech or hold a clinic for some kids or just have dinner in a restaurant where people want autographs and want to say hello to me, I remember that I'm representing what my family is about. I think about things like that all the time.

The sky really is the limit if you put your mind to it. I know that. I've lived it. There were tons of times when those girls were out there calling me a tomboy, making fun of me, getting on my nerves, wanting to fight me, and I could easily have quit, but I didn't. I always had that fire in me. And even when I didn't have that fire— those times when I was cutting school, feeling depressed, caring about nothing—my grandmother was there to guide me and make sure I got back on that right path. Even in situations like the one I had with my parents when I was little. It was awful. Maybe I didn't know or understand everything that was going on, but I was hurt by it. I had a lot of anger and frustration inside. And I know there are a lot of kids out there who have bad relationships with their parents. There are a lot of little kids who go through situations where their parents separate, where their parents aren't there for them.

I can say from experience that it takes time to deal with it, to say to yourself, *I'm going to be mature about this. I'm going to figure out a way.* It took time for me to realize that I can't just run from my problems. It took a long time and strength for me to decide: *I'm going to conquer this. I'm going to figure out a way to have a relationship with my mom.* But eventually I did decide that, and now I feel I've made great strides. We started out slow, simple. She'd always been there, trying to become a part of my life again, and I'd always been the one to push her away. So I decided to stop pushing. Late in my college career, I started accepting her invitations to stay at her house on Staten Island when I came home to New York for a visit—at least, every once in a while. I invited her to come to a few of my games. For me, these were little ways of taking down the wall I'd built between us. It wasn't easy, taking that wall down. It never is for anyone, I suspect, and I am one of those people who is even more cautious. I'd used that wall like a shield against my mother, punishing her for what I felt she'd done to me as a child by keeping her out of my life. Once I let her back in, though, I found out I was a happier person. I have a great relationship with my mom now. And I'm so grateful for that.

I think I learned a lot about myself during my four years in college. When I went to Tennessee it was like going from a ninety-mile-per-hour life to a world that moved forty-five miles per hour. I'm used to going boom, boom, boom! Everything happens at once, and you just deal with it. It was easy for me to get frustrated there, to feel like people had no idea what the outside world was like, to feel like an outsider. But now I recognize that it was God's way of saying, "Chamique, slow down, relax, start to look at things from a different perspective. Enjoy the differences. Enjoy life. Enjoy every minute of it."

You can't live your life afraid you won't fit in, or afraid of failing. You just have to keep practicing, keep working until it feels right. Starting in first grade, I was in all the honors classes, and then in fourth grade, all of a sudden, they moved me down to the second level. That's when I used to sit there at the table in our apartment in Jamaica and my mom would make me do my homework over and over again until it was neat. Until it was perfect. I was talking to my mom about that when I was home recently. I told her I learned something from that. It's a lesson that's valuable to me now, when we're struggling on the Mystics and when I'm playing on this U.S.A. team with all these veterans and I start to feel like I'm making a ton of mistakes because I'm not as smart as they all are or something.

I realize that all I need to do is keep working, and I'll get better and better. Then one day Teresa Edwards walks up to me and says, "See, you're good at this now." That gets me so excited. That's what keeps that fire and that self-confidence going.

There have been so many times in my life when I felt that way, like I wasn't the best at something, or I didn't fit in, or I was going to fail. And it seems like there has always been someone there to believe in me, which makes all the difference. My friends from home. Coach Summitt. Teresa. My grandmother. Mostly, my grandmother. Sure, it's old-fashioned, but that's the one rule I live by: make your family proud. Make your grandmother proud. It's really the only one I need.